FIELD INSTRUCTION

FIELD INSTRUCTION

A GUIDE FOR SOCIAL WORK STUDENTS

DAVID ROYSE

SURJIT SINGH DHOOPER

ELIZABETH LEWIS ROMPF

University of Kentucky, Lexington

Longman

New York & London

Field Instruction: A Guide for Social Work Students

Longman, 10 Bank Street, White Plains, N.Y. 10606

Associated companies:
Longman Group Ltd., London
Longman Cheshire Pty., Melbourne
Longman Paul Pty., Auckland
Copp Clark Pitman, Toronto

Sponsoring editor: David J. Estrin
Development editor: Susan Alkana
Production editor: Victoria Mifsud
Cover design: Joseph DePinho
Text art: Execustaff
Production supervisor: Anne Armeny

Library of Congress Cataloging-in-Publication Data

Royse, David.
    Field instruction : a guide for social work students / David
Royse. Surjit Singh Dhooper, Elizabeth Lewis Rompf.
        p.   cm.
    Includes index.
    ISBN 0-8013-0820-8
    1. Social service—Field work.   I. Dhooper, Surjit Singh.
II. Rompf, Elizabeth Lewis.   III. Title.
HV11.R67   1992
361.3'0723—dc20   92-25387
                                                   CIP

3 4 5 6 7 8 9 10-CRS-97 96 95 94 93

Contents

CHAPTER 5   THE RECIPIENTS OF SERVICE: CLIENTS   59

CHAPTER 6   THE STUDENT INTERN: NEEDED SKILLS   75

Preface

If you are about to begin your first practicum and myriad questions are tumbling around in your head, this book was written for you. It can be thought of as a "survival manual" or "consumer's manual" for students who are beginning their first course in the field. This guide is written primarily for undergraduate students, but most of the material is applicable for graduate students—especially those who cannot draw on their experiences in an undergraduate practicum.

Our intent is to develop a supplemental resource to accompany practicum manuals or materials that social work programs customarily provide to their students. These materials tend to be chiefly concerned with descriptions of social work programs, practicum requirements, and student evaluation processes. Few programs attempt in writing to anticipate students' questions or supply information about the problems most commonly encountered in the field. Undoubtedly, some material provided in this book may be conveyed orally or via handouts to students enrolled in practicum courses, but there is great variation among social work programs and the way their field instruction courses are conceptualized and administered.

We have tried to be comprehensive but succinct. This guide is not intended to replace texts that generally are used with social work foundation courses. For some important topics, the discussion is designed to be a quick refresher of what students probably already know. Students, faculty, or field instructors who want more detailed coverage should consult the references at the end of each chapter.

We believe that this book is necessary because field instruction has such an important place in social work education. Field instruction (also known as field work, field experience, practicum, or internship) makes textbook learning come alive by providing students with opportunities to apply the theories and processes learned in class to real life situations. Besides consolidating and reinforcing your classroom instruction, a practicum allows the occasion to test your interest in working with clients who are mentally ill, homeless, alcoholic, pregnant, impoverished, or victims of child abuse or domestic violence.

Many of you will have a faculty person who coordinates and oversees your practicum experience. Within your program, these individuals may be known as faculty supervisors, field coordinators, seminar instructors, faculty advisers, faculty consultants, or faculty field liaisons. Depending on the social work program, their role may be chiefly that of initially helping you to find an appropriate agency, or they may be quite involved—frequently making contact with you or the agency to stay apprised of your progress. Although their titles vary greatly from university to university, we will always refer to them here as *faculty field liaisons*. You may need to make this mental conversion if they are called something different in your program. Similarly, persons supervising students in the field can be known as agency supervisors, field supervisors, intern supervisors, or field instructors. Of these terms, we use *agency supervisors* and *field instructors* interchangeably.

Most students find the practicum to be a valuable experience that confirms they have made the right career choice. Still, the responsibility associated with being in an unfamiliar agency and being assigned genuine clients may make some students a little anxious and unsure of themselves. Even confident students have questions prior to and during their field experiences. By offering practical advice to some commonly raised questions, we hope to reduce your anxiety so that you can maximize your learning and development as a social work professional. We want you to be informed and competent and to have a good experience in becoming a professional within our social service delivery system!

David Royse
Surjit Singh Dhooper
Elizabeth Lewis Rompf

FIELD INSTRUCTION

CHAPTER 1

Field Instruction and the Social Work Curriculum

Overview

This introductory chapter provides the historical and current context for understanding the requirement of field instruction in social work programs. It also begins to answer questions about student preparation, supervision, and the coordination of field instruction within the larger educational program.

Why Do Social Work Students Have Field Instruction?

As professionals in the making, social work students attend classes to learn practice principles, values and ethical behaviors, a body of specialized knowledge, and the scientific basis for practice. In field instruction, students apply what they learn in the classroom to real situations. Thus, the preparation to become a social work professional is composed of formal learning as well as practical experience. Practicums or internships are not unique to social work but are common to most of the helping professions.

A career in social work requires many different types of competence. Social workers must have competence in relating to people as individuals, in groups, and in communities; in assessing needs and problems; and in planning and intervening appropriately. Social workers have to be skilled in carrying out various helping roles such as advocate, broker, educator, mediator, clinician, community planner and organizer, administrator, and so forth. While students may not be able to acquire competence in each of these roles during a single practicum, placement in an agency allows them the opportunity to observe other professionals and to learn from their actions. Students can learn from any of the staff around them—all play a role in helping students to become more proficient.

As students obtain practical experience from the field, they are socialized into the professional subculture. Briggs (1977) suggests two aspects of this socialization: The first is the acceptance of individuals into a professional group and conformity with expectations held of all members, and the second is the development within the individuals of a professional self-concept consistent with role models. During field instruction, encounters with clients, colleagues, and the professional community help to educate and indoctrinate students into the culture, norms, and values of social work (Briggs, 1977). Field instruction assists students in making the transition from passive learners to active professionals.

Field instruction is a valuable part of the social work curriculum because it allows students an occasion to determine whether or not social work is the best career for them. The choice of a career is a major decision, and not everyone is suited to be a social worker. Because students are closely supervised and evaluated, faculty field liaisons can help students identify their strengths and weaknesses and determine whether or not social work is the best choice for them.

What Is the History of Field Instruction in Social Work?

Field instruction has always been a major part of social work training. Its history goes back to the days of the Charity Organization Societies in the last quarter of the nineteenth century, when students learned social work by apprenticeship. Through "applied philanthropy" students obtained firsthand knowledge of poverty and adverse social conditions. With this apprenticeship model, training emphasized "doing" and deriving knowledge from that activity. By the end of the nineteenth century, social work was moving away from the apprenticeship model.

The first training school for social work was a summer program that opened in 1898 at the New York City Charity Organization Society. In 1904, the society established the New York School of Philanthropy, which offered an 8-month instructional program. Mary Richmond, an early social work practitioner, teacher, and theoretician, argued that although many learned by doing, this type of learning must be supplemented by theory. She called for a permanent group of instructors to direct the work of students, to give them theory and practice together (George, 1982).

At the 1915 National Conference of Charities and Corrections, presenters emphasized the value of an educationally based field-practice experience, with schools of social work having control over students' learning assignments. This idea put schools in the position of exercising authority over the selection of agencies for field training and thus control over the quality of social work practice to which students were exposed.

Early in social work education a pattern was established whereby students spent roughly half of their academic time in field settings selected by the school of social work with the school overseeing the students' experiences (Austin, 1986). This paradigm was made possible by the networking that emerged from the early organizational efforts of social work educators. For instance, in 1919 the Organization of the Association of Training Schools for Professional Social Work was chartered by 17 programs. By 1923, 13 of the original 17 schools were associated with universities or colleges at the postbaccalaureate level. The American Association of Schools of Social Work, in its curriculum standards of 1932, formally recognized field instruction as an essential part of social work education (Mesbur, 1991).

During the first part of this century, psychoanalytic theory dominated social work education. This influence tended to focus the attention of students and social work educators on a client's personality rather than on the social environment. Accordingly, social casework as learned in the practicum emphasized helping the individual more than bringing about social justice or social reform (Sikkema, 1966).

The depression of the 1930s and the enactment of the Social Security Act of 1935 brought about major changes in the country's provision of social services and need for social workers.

During the period from about 1940 until 1960, an academic approach dominated social work education. This approach emphasized students' cognitive development and knowledge-directed practice. Professors expected students to deduce practice approaches from classroom learning and translate theories into functional behaviors in the field (Tolson & Kopp, 1988). Curriculum policies in 1944 and in 1952 led toward the gradual acceptance of social work as a two-year professional educational program.

Educational standards for field instruction were refined in the 1940s and the 1950s, and field work became known as field instruction. A subcommittee on field work for the American Association of Schools of Social Work (the forerunner of the Council on Social Work Education) took the position in 1940–1941 that field teaching was just as important as classroom teaching and demanded equally qualified teachers and definite criteria for the selection of field agencies (Reynolds, 1965).

The *articulated approach* characterized the third phase in the history of social work field instruction (from about 1960 to the present). This method integrates features of both the experiential approach and the academic approach. It is concerned with a planned relationship between cognitive and experiential learning. It requires that both class and field learning be developed with learning objectives carefully sequenced to allow for their integration. It does not demand that students be inductive or deductive learners but keep knowledge development and practice close enough together in time to minimize these differences in learning style (Jenkins & Sheafor, 1982). During this phase, the Council on Social Work Education was formed in 1952. It established and revised standards for institutions granting degrees in social work. These standards required a clear plan for the organization, implementation, and evaluation of both in-class work and the field practicum. The 1982 Curriculum Policy Statement further emphasized academic control of educational experiences in field instruction as distinct from an apprenticeship model of training (Austin, 1986).

Today, social work programs vary in the type of field experience provided (e.g., block, concurrent) and in the number of hours of field instruction required. However, there is virtually no disagreement among social work educators as to the educational emphasis that should be placed on field instruction and the importance of it being highly integrated with theoretical and knowledge-based instructional courses.

What Are the Current Standards for Field Instruction?

The Council on Social Work Education requires that undergraduate programs provide each student with a minimum of 400 hours of field instruction. Graduate programs must arrange a minimum of 900 hours. The council further stipulates that the practicum be a clearly designed educational experience and that social work programs have articulated standards for selecting agencies for practicum, for selecting field instructors (agency supervisors), and for evaluating student learning in the practicum. You may find that your particular program requires more field instruction than the minimum expected by the council. This works to your advantage because more experience gives you a greater chance to refine your skills and to develop expertise.

Are There Different Types of Field Placement?

Social work programs can organize the required field instruction in different ways as long as they are educationally directed, coordinated, monitored, and meet the requirements of the Council on Social Work Education. The most common types of field placements are block and concurrent. Under the *block* placement arrangement, a student is placed in a social service agency with an approved learning plan for a block of time—a whole academic term, two full terms, or a summer term. The students devote full time (4 or 5 days per week) to experiential learning from assignments in the agency. Under a *modified block model* students participate in field instruction in a social service agency 4 days each week while the 5th day is reserved for taking courses.

Under the *concurrent* placement, the students' time is divided between classroom learning and field work experiences. (Typically, students are expected to be in the agency for 2 or 3 days per week and to take classes for 2 or 3 days.) The exact proportion of time devoted to each set of learning experiences varies, depending on the type of academic term, the number of academic credits, and whether or not the students are undergraduates or 1st- or 2nd-year graduate students.

Social work programs across the country have mixed and matched these two types of placements to create different models of field instruction. For example, Florida State University's School of Social Work and the University of Louisville's Kent School of Social Work require their 1st-year graduate students to do a *concurrent placement* (2 days per week for two semesters) and their 2nd-year students to complete a block placement (for 15 weeks at 5 days per week). Fordham University's Graduate School of Social Service offers three models of field practicum: the *standard model*—two years of concurrent placements for 28 weeks each year at 3 days (21 hours) per week; the *extended model*—two years of concurrent placement for 42 weeks each year at 2 days (14 hours) per week; and the Reduced Field Instruction Model—one year of placement for 33 weeks at 4 days (28 hours) per week (Council on Social Work Education, 1991).

How Are Students Prepared for Field Instruction?

At the undergraduate level, social work programs prepare students for beginning generalist social work practice with individuals, families, groups, and communities. To reach this objective, most programs follow a three-step graduated approach. At step 1, generally in their sophomore or junior year, students enroll in a practice course that consists of lectures (or seminars), classroom assignments, and often several hours of volunteer work each week in a human service agency. The volunteer work encourages familiarity with networks of human service programs—the structure of agencies, the community services, and the requirements for being an agency worker (Johnson, 1988). This course is often referred to as a *miniplacement*, and students receive 3 or 4 academic credit hours for it. The time spent in this minipracticum cannot be counted toward the Council on Social Work Education's minimum requirement of 400 clock hours in the field practicum.

Step 2 is the completion of basic core courses—social work practice, human behavior and the social environment, social welfare policy and services, and social research. Step 3 is the placement of students in their field practicum. Faculty field liaisons assign students to social welfare agencies so that they can acquire new skills and further refine their existing skills. In many programs, the practicum is scheduled for the senior year.

Undergraduates may be required to be in the field agency for 4 days per week for about 30 clock hours. Some programs require two practicum courses, thus going well beyond the 400-minimum-clock-hour requirement of the Council on Social Work Education. In these programs, students may take some of their core courses along with their first practicum.

How Are Practicum Students Supervised?

In most programs, students are placed in a community service agency under the day-to-day supervision of a field instructor who is a social worker employed by the agency. It is the responsibility of the field instructor to provide students with opportunities for client contact and to oversee students' performance with assigned tasks. Field instructors are considered members of the extended teaching staff of the school and may be granted faculty privileges such as the use of the university library facilities or receive discounts at the university bookstore.

Field instructors are well aware of the social work program's philosophy, the content and sequence of courses, and the expected level of student performance. Often there are special training sessions for new field instructors—this ensures that assignments given to students are consistent with students' abilities and the program's expectations. In addition to the supervision students receive from field instructors, social work programs usually assign faculty members as advisers to students and as liaisons between the agency and the school.

Students should realize that social work programs vary considerably from school to school (and sometimes even within a school) in terms of the level of student monitoring that field liaisons do. Some faculty field liaisons will meet with their students weekly but with their field instructors at the beginning of the term, at the midpoint, and at the end of the term—other faculty field liaisons will meet with field instructors only for an evaluation at the end of the term. Some faculty will monitor students' progress by requiring written or oral assignments (e.g., case presentations, planned observations, or interviews); others do not. Even though your field instructor may be asked for a recommendation regarding the grade you earned in your practicum, the assignment of the grade is most often the responsibility of the faculty field liaison.

What Is the Role of the Faculty Field Liaison?

The primary job of the faculty field liaison is to see that students' practicum experiences are educational. Rosenblum and Raphael (1983) describe specific faculty field liaison's duties as (1) facilitating field teaching and students' learning, (2) monitoring educational opportunities offered by the agency and students' progress, and fostering an interchange between school and agency, and (3) evaluating field instructors' efforts and students' achievements. Faria, Brownstein, and Smith (1988) identify 10 liaison responsibilities, which they divide into six roles and four functions. The liaison roles are:

> *Adviser*—provides assistance to students in planning for practicum. (This includes identifying learning needs and educational experiences to meet those needs.)
>
> *Monitor*—assesses agencies, field instructors, and students' learning experiences. (This would include reviewing and approving students' learning agreement.)
>
> *Consultant*—assists field instructors in developing supervisory skills and providing course outlines and other materials.
>
> *Teacher*—assists students with the integration of course work and practicum, and serves as a role model to students.
>
> *Mediator*—assists in resolving problems between students and field instructors or other agency personnel.
>
> *Advocate*—provides relevant information to academic review committees (when necessary) to evaluate students' field and academic performance.

The faculty field liaison functions are:

> *Practicum placement*—selects field agencies and field instructors, and matches them with students' learning needs.
>
> *Linkage*—interprets school policies, procedures, and expectations of field agencies, and assesses the fit between school curriculum and educational experiences provided by the agency.

Evaluation—evaluates students, field instructors, and agencies; assigns students' grades; and makes recommendations for continued use of agencies and field instructors.

Administration—ensures completion of placement forms (e.g., students' evaluation of agencies, field instructors, and faculty field liaisons).

Often the faculty field liaisons have ongoing relationships with the same agencies for a number of years and become quite familiar with them and their staff who serve as field supervisors for the students. In some places, faculty field liaisons work exclusively with a group of agencies within a select field of practice (e.g., health and mental health).

In many programs, faculty field liaisons conduct required weekly seminars to help with integrating theory and practice. Seminars provide students with a regular occasion to share their learning and to ask for information or assistance when difficult problems arise. In addition, students may be expected to submit weekly logs of their field experiences and have individual conferences with their faculty field liaisons. These conferences provide more opportunities for coordination between the university and the field agency and for integration of theory and practice. Through all of these efforts, the faculty field liaison attempts to assist the student, the field instructor, and the agency in meeting the educational objectives established for the student's field instruction.

How Are Classroom Learning and Field Instruction Integrated?

The very nature of field instruction fosters integration with classroom learning. Students will often comment on how some new material learned in one class can be used with a particular client. Or, students may share with their classmates some aspects of an interesting case they have been assigned in their practicum. Social work programs have also employed a variety of approaches to nurture integration. These have ranged from "the creation of faculty-headed field units in existing agencies and the development of school-community learning service centers to the establishment of university-based practicum opportunities" (Rosenblum & Raphael, 1983, p. 67).

Still other programs try to ensure integration of course material and field instruction indirectly by creating and maintaining a harmonious collaborative relationship between the school and the field agency. For example, faculty may conduct in-service training or workshops in the field agencies, include field instructors on advisory boards to provide feedback on the field education component, or hold appreciation dinners or receptions for field instructors. Occasionally, students ask their field instructors to travel to the university to speak to a particular class. Whenever the faculty of social work programs and the staff of field agencies hosting student interns meet and discuss mutual concerns, opportunities arise to explore ways to integrate students' field experiences with classroom learning.

Efforts to achieve integration can also be more purposive, as when agency field instructors supervising students for the first time are required to attend seminars on field instruction, which may extend over several weeks, conducted by the social work faculty. Topics may include orientation of students to agencies, supervision, practicum-related policies and procedures, selection of student assignments, use of student recordings, teaching concepts and methodology, and evaluation processes. Even though orientation programs for field instructors vary widely, these sessions facilitate the integration of field and classroom experiences as field instructors are given access to course outlines, bibliographies, curriculum statements, field manuals, newsletters, and other relevant documents. In such orientations, the expectations of faculty members can be clearly stated.

Most social work programs place the major responsibility for the integration of classroom learning and field instruction on the faculty field liaison. As discussed earlier, the faculty field liaison may use methods such as integrating field seminars, commenting on students' logs, or holding conferences with students to increase the integration of classroom and field experiences.

However, the students' roles should not be overlooked. Students can enrich their learning by sharing information from their courses or from relevant research that they have come across with their field instructors, and by making a point to bring into the classroom their interesting field experiences, discussions, cases, and learning from their agencies. Equally valuable is the habit of reflecting on what is being learned in the field. Students should periodically ask themselves questions such as, What knowledge, skills, or values am I learning in field? How appropriate are the theories that I have learned in class for understanding and working with my assigned cases? In what areas are the theories underdeveloped? How do situations encountered with real clients provide realistic examples of core course content? Such reflection, practiced from time to time, would not only help students to integrate classroom content and field education, but also promote students' growth as active, responsible, self-directed learners.

Do Students with Undergraduate Field Instruction Get Credit When They Work toward a Master's Degree in Social Work?

Yes. Most Master of Social Work (MSW) programs allow applicants with Bachelor of Social Work (BSW) degrees from schools accredited by the Council on Social Work Education to apply for *advanced standing* status. If given this status, students are usually granted a waiver allowing them to bypass one term of field experience. Students with undergraduate degrees in social work from accredited programs often waive about one-fourth of the overall credits required for a master's degree.

Although the basic qualification for the waiver is graduation from an accredited undergraduate social work program, most programs also insist that applicants earn at least a "B" average in their social work courses. Decisions are made on an individual basis. Some programs also require a written qualifying examination covering foundation course material and a personal interview. A few schools (e.g., Case Western Reserve University's School of Applied Social Sciences) grant 15 hours of credit that may be applied to their required courses by passing an examination, or may be used as electives without taking the examination. In other programs, advanced standing students are required to begin the program in a particular semester or quarter. For example, the University of Denver's Graduate School of Social Work requires advanced standing students to begin in a summer session and continue full time through three terms of the following year.

Is It Possible for a Graduate Student to Have a Placement Where He or She Is Also Employed?

The answer is a qualified yes. Although this option is not routinely available to undergraduates, graduate programs do occasionally allow students to be placed in the same agencies where they are employed when certain conditions are met. Not all employment situations qualify. Students are to be employed in agencies meeting all field instruction and other program standards and expectations. Other requirements often include having different responsibilities from those customarily performed, having a different MSW supervisor from the regular supervisor, and receiving permission from the employing agency for release from paid duties during regular business hours in order to be a student.

The best rationale for requesting a practicum in the agency where one is employed is the availability of unique educational experiences—exposure to a clientele or intervention not available at any other agency. Some agencies also encourage their employees to "cross-train" so that they have a pool of better qualified and experienced staff on which to draw. These agencies may be willing to provide release time in order for student-employees to learn different skills within the agency. The concern that most faculty field liaisons have with allowing students to have a practicum with an employer is that it may be difficult for the students to be viewed as "learners" by the student-employees' colleagues. Because of their knowledge of the agency and its programs, these students may be given so much responsibility that they are unable to read, study, or reflect on their new practice experiences. As a result, these students may be so busy (especially if not given release time) that they are unable to differentiate hours spent as a regular employee and time spent as a student intern.

In our experience, large agencies (such as hospitals) provide the best models for situations where students could be both employees and students. For instance, Sue could be a hospital social worker assigned full time to the maternity unit. If a practicum within the psychiatric unit could be worked out, she would have different responsibilities and supervision. When working in the maternity unit, it would be clear that Sue was functioning as an employee, and when working in the psychiatric unit, Sue would be functioning in the student role.

IDEAS FOR ENRICHING YOUR
PRACTICUM EXPERIENCE

1. Go to the library and see if you can find any historical material on the agency or type of agency where you will or would like to be placed as a student intern. Also, find and read one of the several excellent books on the early years of the Hull House.

2. Interview a student who has just completed a practicum or a retired social worker and ask this person to describe the most valuable lesson that he or she learned in a practicum or while practicing as a social worker.

3. How long has the social work program been provided at your college or university? What local agencies were involved and supportive at its start? What were practicums like when the program first started, and how have they changed? Ask the social work librarian or reference librarian to help you find material to answer these questions.

4. Find the yellow pages of your telephone directory where social service agencies are listed. Can you identify public and private agencies? How many of the agencies have names that make it difficult to know the population or type of problem with which they work? How many of the agencies are you familiar with? How many are you encountering for the first time?

5. Take a moment to reflect on the type of cases or community problems that you will encounter during this practicum. Can you think of a question or an issue that would make interesting discussion in a social policy class? Have you identified any problems for which there doesn't seem to be any research in the social work literature? How does what you have learned in your practice or human behavior courses apply to the types of problems you see or expect to see in your practicum?

6. How many fields of service can you identify where social workers are typically employed? List as many as you can and then check this list against the areas of service identified in *Social Work Research and Abstracts,* published by the National Association of Social Workers in Washington, D.C.

7. What are your particular strengths, abilities, and talents? How can you most effectively communicate these to your new field instructor?

CASE VIGNETTE TO STIMULATE YOUR THINKING

John at 23 years of age has changed college majors five times in the past 3 years. He entered as an English literature major, then changed to accounting. In his sophomore year he tried geography and Russian. After one year of Russian, he decided against continuing with this major and dropped out of school to "get his act together." You would suspect that John uses a lot of drugs. At a minimum, he drinks too much. This fall, he entered again as a psychology major but has only taken the introductory course. Hearing your excitement as you make plans to begin a practicum at the American Red Cross convinces John that he, too, ought to become a social work major although he is not well informed about the type of settings that employ social workers or the role of a professional social worker. He says that he never has liked sitting in a classroom. The idea of working on his own in an agency and getting university credits for it is very appealing to him.

QUESTIONS

What questions could you ask John to help him examine his motivations and values before hastily deciding to change majors?

Why, in your mind, should a person choose the career of a social worker?

What characteristics make a good social worker?

How likely is it that John will be able to work without any supervision?

REFERENCES

Austin, D. M. (1986). *A history of social work education.* Austin, TX: University of Texas at Austin, School of Social Work.

Briggs, T. L. (1977). The role of field instruction in achieving the manifest and latent functions of professional education. In T. L. Briggs & G. M. Gross (Eds.), *Field instruction: New perspectives on partnership.* Syracuse, NY: School of Social Work, Manpower Monograph No. 12.

Council on Social Work Education. (1991). *Summary information on master of social work programs, 1990.* Alexandria, VA: Author.

Faria, G., Brownstein, C., & Smith, H. Y. (1988). A survey of field instructors' perceptions of the liaison role. *Journal of Social Service Education, 24*(2), 135–144.

George, A. (1982). A history of social work field instruction: Apprenticeship to instruction. In B. W. Sheafor & L. E. Jenkins (Eds.), *Quality field instruction in social work.* White Plains, NY: Longman.

Jenkins, L. E., & Sheafor, B. W. (1982). An overview of social work field instruction. In B. W. Sheafor & L. E. Jenkins (Eds.), *Quality field instruction in social work.* White Plains, NY: Longman.

Johnson, H. W. (1988). Volunteer work in the introductory course: A special curriculum component. *Journal of Social Work Education, 24*(2), 145–150.

Mesbur, E. S. (1991). Overview of baccalaureate field instruction: Objectives and outcomes. In D. Schneck, B. Grossman, & U. Glassman (Eds.), *Field instruction in social work: Contemporary issues and trends.* Dubuque, IA: Kendall/Hunt.

Reynolds, B. C. (1965). *Learning and teaching in the practice of social work.* New York: Russell & Russell.

Rosenblum, A. F., & Raphael, F. B. (1983). The role and function of the faculty field liaison. *Journal of Education for Social Work, 19*(1), 67–73.

Sikkema, M. (1966). A proposal for an innovation in field learning. In *Field instruction in graduate social work education: Old problems and new proposals.* New York: Council on Social Work Education.

Tolson, E. R., & Kopp, J. (1988). The practicum: Clients, problems, interventions, and influences on student practice. *Journal of Social Work Education, 24*(2), 123–134.

ADDITIONAL READINGS

Council on Social Work Education. (1966). *Field instruction in graduate school work education.* New York: Author.

Family Service Association of America. (1966). *Trends in field work instruction.* New York: Author.

Gilbert, N., & Specht, H. (1981). *Handbook of the social services.* Englewood Cliffs, NJ: Prentice-Hall.

Lauffer, A. (1984). *Understanding your social agency.* Beverly Hills, CA: Sage Publications.
———. (1987). *Working in social work: Growing and thriving in human services practice.* Newbury Park, CA: Sage Publications.
Siporin, M. (1982). The process of field instruction. In B. W. Sheafor & L. E. Jenkins (Eds.), *Quality field instruction in social work* (pp. 175–197). White Plains, NY: Longman.
Skolnik, L. (1989). Field instruction in the 1980s: Realities, issues, and problem-solving strategies. In M. S. Raskin (Ed.), *Empirical studies in field instruction.* New York: Haworth Press.
White, H. R. (1988). Pros and cons of student placements with employers. *ARETE, 13*(2), 50–54.

CHAPTER 2

The Partnership with Social Service Agencies

Overview

The intention of this chapter is to answer basic questions about social service agencies and field instructors who host and supervise social work students during their field instruction.

Why Do Agencies Accept Student Interns?

Social service agencies rarely receive direct financial incentives from universities to provide field experiences for university students. However, these agencies like being affiliated with universities—the training of students is stimulating and enriching for both the agency staff and the students involved. And, there are secondary benefits. Social service agencies tend to be tremendously underfunded and often have too many clients and too few staff. When there are not enough staff in an agency, students provide important and valued help. By using students to assist them, social work staff can sometimes focus on more problematic cases, or begin projects that have been put aside for lack of time. You should expect that the tasks assigned to you will be helpful to the agency. The assignments given to students normally are selected because they meet specific learning objectives and introduce students to the variety of tasks performed by social workers in the practicum setting.

Also, it would be atypical for a social service agency not to have a strong commitment to the training and development of future social workers. The agency not only contributes to increasing the number and quality of social work professionals, but also finds that providing placements for students has two other advantages: First, the agency is able to screen, orient, train, and evaluate potential job applicants with a minimal investment in personnel costs. (When there are staff positions vacant, it is not unusual for student interns to be offered employment by the agency.)

Second, even if the agency cannot offer employment, it benefits by having a pool of potential applicants in the community who are knowledgeable about the agency's services. Even though former practicum students will take jobs in other agencies, they will be in positions where they can make referrals to the practicum agency and, in general, will serve as public relations agents—increasing the agency's visibility in the community.

Beyond these reasons, staff within an agency may advocate for a practicum setting. Staff who volunteer to supervise students do so because they enjoy teaching. They may find that their own practice skills are sharpened as they discuss with students various aspects of their practice. Furthermore, working with students can expose the agency staff to new developments in social work and help to relieve job fatigue.

How Are Field Agencies Chosen?

There are several paths by which a human service agency may become a field instruction site for social work students. A faculty member, a social work practitioner in the community, or a student may recommend an agency. An agency may contact a social work program and request students. Or, agencies may be approached directly by a faculty field liaison. Generally, agencies are expected to provide information on their programs, the learning experiences available to students, and the qualifications of the personnel available to supervise students. Faculty field liaisons look for agencies whose programs have competent staff to provide effective supervision and professional learning; a commitment to social work ethics, values, and the training of social work professionals; diverse and broad programs compatible with the school's educational objectives; and adequate physical facilities (e.g., desk space, telephone access) to accommodate students.

Even agencies that meet these general criteria may not become field agencies. Often, other factors such as the agency's reputation in the community, its leadership or innovation, and its climate (whether it is conducive to student learning) are considered. Some of the agencies that meet the above general criteria may become particularly attractive as field instruction sites because of considerations such as method of intervention, problem area of practice, population served, or availability of stipends for students.

After an agency has been found suitable for field instruction, the school and the agency frequently enter into a formal contractual agreement governing placement of students. Contained in the contract are the conditions, expectations, and terms of agreement that are to be in effect during the course of a student's practicum.

Some social work programs recommend that each field agency develop an outline for field instruction detailing important orientation items, assignments, and learning opportunities. Most social work programs maintain files of agency data to which students have easy access.

How Are Field Instructors Selected?

Although agency executive directors may recommend certain staff as supervisors for students, the faculty field liaison ultimately has the responsibility for determining who will supervise the university's students. Criteria often include a master's degree from an accredited social work program and 2 to 3 years of postgraduate degree professional experience in a given practice area. It is also desirable that the field instructor have at least 6 months of experience within the particular agency. In some settings, the field instructor may be an experienced BSW. Beyond these minimal requirements, the faculty field liaison looks for field instructors who have an interest in teaching and who are supportive of students. Field instructors have to be both knowledgeable and flexible individuals. They need to make time for overseeing students and for coordinating with faculty field liaisons. Field instructors tend to be among the most competent and energetic of an agency's staff. They incorporate the values and ethics of the profession and usually make excellent role models for students.

In order to know that field instructors meet the minimum requirements, social work programs usually gather curricula vitae and maintain a file on supervisors. However, just meeting the minimum requirements does not make a "good" field instructor. When field instructors give students too little of their time, make unrealistic demands, or in other ways show themselves unable to assist students in their educational endeavors, these field instructors tend not to be used again.

How Are Agencies and Students Matched?

Frequently, students will have a preference for specific practicum settings. Some students know that they want to work with older adults when they graduate and desire to begin refining their skills with this population. Other students know that they want to work with children or in a medical setting. We believe (although there does not appear to be any research on this topic) that the majority of faculty field liaisons attempt to place students in a practicum that would be consistent with the students' first or second choice. However, there are undoubtedly faculty field liaisons who believe that student input is less important than other considerations.

Assuming that you have a preference (e.g., a mental health setting) and that your faculty field liaison will attempt to find you a practicum within this general area, what additional considerations are important? In our experience, faculty field liaisons give first consideraton to the student's educational and learning needs. Faculty field liaisons must assess each student's specific needs and familiarity with the field of social work. Students who are knowledgeable or experienced in one area or type of agency should expect that they will be exposed to new activities (e.g., case management or advocacy) in an effort to help them to become well rounded. Students who want to dedicate all of their practicum experience to a specific population (e.g., psychiatric outpatients in a private practice clinic) may find that not every program will support this specialization. Philosophically, many faculty field liaisons believe that at least the first practicum ought to expose the student to a broad array of diverse clients. This is particularly true in undergraduate practicums and generalist graduate programs.

Students who either have been employed in social service agencies or have extensive volunteer experience will generally be given placements where greater responsibility, knowledge, or judgment are required. Students who have had very little or no exposure to social services will often be assigned to agencies where lack of previous experience will not be a disadvantage or a disservice to clients.

Less experienced students are not necessarily placed in situations where there will be limited exposure to clients—these students can still expect significant contact with clients, but in settings where there will be ample structure and supervision (e.g., assisting in a day treatment program for the chronically mentally ill). More experienced students will be able to function in situations where there is less structure or direct supervision. An example would be a respite program for senior citizens where (after a brief orientation period) students would be expected to travel to clients' homes to conduct assessments for the program.

In making assignments to agencies, faculty field liaisons also consider the individual student. It is very likely that a student who gives the appearance of being unorganized, immature, or irresponsible will be placed in a less challenging practicum than a student considered organized, mature, and responsible. Of course, other traits or characteristics may also influence the faculty field liaison's decision. For instance, a confident and assertive student might be placed in a setting such as a locked psychiatric ward of a large hospital before a timid student would be.

Another factor that affects the placement of students has to do with the faculty field liaison's contacts in the community. A faculty field liaison who is well known in the community may receive requests for students from local social service agencies. These requests can be rather specific. An agency with a shortage of male therapists might request a male student who enjoys working with adolescents. An after-school or day treatment program for children might request a student who is athletic and able to participate in strenuous sports such as swimming and backpacking. If you are a student with prior experience in scouting, recreational programming, or camping, the faculty field liaison may see you first in terms of meeting the agency's request. Faculty field liaisons know it is important to find students who meet social service agencies' needs so that the training opportunities afforded by these agencies will continue to be available to future social work students. Such considerations may be responsible for students' not getting their first but a second or third choice of a practicum.

What Specifically Are Social Service Agencies Looking for in Student Interns?

When interviewing students who are seeking practicum placements, agency supervisors tend to look for several characteristics: First is a strong desire on the part of the student to help others. Second is the student's interest and ability to deal with specific knowledge and skills relative to particular problem areas. Third is emotional maturity. Each of these will be briefly discussed.

A Strong Desire to Help Others.   Most agency supervisors believe that the basic quality practicum students must have is a burning desire to help others. This desire should be a driving force in students' lives—they must feel it enough to keep trying even when it appears that a client wants to fail. Students must have a high tolerance for frustration and be unwilling to accept a no answer. Social work can be discouraging, and students must be strongly motivated by the belief that clients want to help themselves. One agency supervisor explained,

> It is crucial to have the ability to be empathic with clients—to genuinely believe that clients are good people. Social workers must believe that clients love their children, they hate being out of work, they value being appreciated, and expect the usual human courtesies. Without these qualities there is no way to make a social worker out of a person.

Agencies are looking for students who are determined, enthusiastic, and have genuine empathy for people. When a student displays attitudes that are indicative of condescension, you can be sure empathy is lacking. Students with empathy are easy to talk with, are good listeners, are not cynical. They understand the client's world and the meaning it has for the client, both cognitively and emotionally.

> The client perceives the [student] acting in response to empathetic understanding when, in the client's words, "He was able to see and feel things in exactly the same way I do." "Many of the things she said just seemed to hit the nail on the head." "He understood my words but also how I felt." "When I did not know what I meant at all clearly, she still understood me." (Kadushin, 1972, p. 52)

Interest and Ability to Function in a Particular Setting.   Agency interviewers seek students with genuine interest in the problem areas with which their organization deals. For example, an interest in addiction treatment is best displayed by a genuine desire to understand the human experience of addiction, not merely an understanding of the theories about addiction. Agencies do not want students who are fascinated by the complexity of a problem (e.g., multiple personality disorder) but lack empathy for the person with the disorder. A few students may be screened out when it is apparent that what really interests them is the disorder, not the living, breathing person involved. Agencies want a student whose concern is for a fellow human being, motivated by *both* an intellectual curiosity about the problem and a compassionate desire to help.

Particularly at the graduate level, agency supervisors may look for knowledge and skills in specific areas. For instance, for the problem of addiction, students must understand the disease model. Beyond this, agency supervisors may expect students to be able to recognize concepts such as transference and countertransference. Although it takes many years of practice to deal with countertransference, the foundations of these skills can be assessed long before students reach any degree of proficiency. This may be done by asking students about past experiences in which they felt frustrated or sad in relating to other people who had problems of any sort.

Maturity.   Many agency supervisors try to assess the intellectual and emotional maturity displayed by a practicum applicant. Maturity is difficult to examine; however, some qualities serve as indicators. Intellectually and emotionally mature individuals have achieved a balance between self-directed activity and a knowledge about the limitations of their competence. This is frequently displayed when applicants have formulated some clear objectives and are willing to seek advice from others about what might be of importance and interest. Furthermore, it is displayed by what Suzuki (1970) called the *beginner's mind.* This is a mind that is inquisitive and open but not cluttered with opinion and prejudice. This quality is apparent when applicants are unafraid to ask fundamental questions and question fundamental assumptions.

Finally, maturity is demonstrated when students are willing to learn from a broad range of individuals and recognize that the field instructor is not the only source of information and guidance. At the same time, mature students do not shop around for better advice than what their supervisors have given.

Although agencies have certain expectations about the qualities students need to possess prior to beginning an internship, for perhaps the majority of agencies the attitudes and values you bring to the interview will be more important than any specific skills or knowledge you have acquired in your education.

How Will the Agency Evaluate My Performance as a Student Intern?

Although there is a lot of variation in the evaluation procedures used by different agencies and social work programs, you can expect that your field instructor will be looking at your progress during the placement. Field instructors often use prepared forms or scales to rate students on their knowledge, skills, and social work values. These forms may be supplied by your faculty field liaison or may have been developed at the agency. Field instructors will orally discuss their written evaluations with students or will give students the opportunity to review their comments and respond. In some programs, faculty field liaisons attend the evaluation session. During your orientation to the agency or to the field practicum, you may be given a copy of the evaluation form that will be used. If a copy is not supplied, ask for one so that you can be familiar with the areas in which you will be expected to show improvement. Alternatively, you could review the sample forms contained in Wilson's (1981) book *Field Instruction,* because many programs use forms that are similar to or modified from the ones Wilson prepared. (More discussion of this topic is provided in Chapter 4.)

In addition to the skills and knowledge you are expected to acquire, certain other qualities are necessary: Foremost are having good attendance and being on time for your appointments and scheduled workdays. You may be thought to be unreliable if your attendance is poor (even if you have good excuses). Other qualities that agencies like in student interns include a pleasant disposition, willingness to work (sometimes expressed as interest in helping others when not busy with your own assignments), a sense of humor, sensible (businesslike) appearance, and sincerity in learning. Furthermore, agencies want students who are in control of their emotions, who are calm and objective (even under stressful conditions), who have good judgment, and who are appropriately assertive.

Most field instructors will rate more highly those student interns who have qualities that would make them good employees once the practicum is finished. As suggested earlier, these would be individuals who get along easily with their co-workers and clients, who are hard working, conscientious, and responsible. Student interns who are willing to help out no matter what the task, and those considered to be an asset to the agency (perhaps because they have developed a special expertise or have found a niche for themselves in the agency), are favored by field instructors and agency administrators.

Here are some other guidelines to help you get along with your field instructor and other staff within the agency:

- Don't try to impress fellow co-workers with vocabulary that you have just learned in your classes.
- When you communicate in writing, use good grammar and spelling and try to write legibly. (If you are a poor speller, use a dictionary to check what you have written.)
- Listen carefully to any instructions given to you the first time and make notes if necessary. Do not make a practice of going back to the agency supervisor on multiple occasions to ask for information that has already been given to you. However, if you need further instructions or information to complete your assignments, then it is more responsible to ask for help than to finish an assignment incorrectly.
- Don't give your field instructor the impression that you are picky about the assignments you will take. If you are not being given enough work, don't be afraid to ask for additional duties.
- Once you have been given responsibility for something, then carry it out. Don't draw out tasks; don't forget assignments.
- Be on time and keep appointments.
- If you borrow something, then return it. Show consideration to others. Don't leave a mess for others to clean.
- If there are personality clashes or personnel problems within the agency, try not to get involved. Avoid agency gossip or discussion that you perceive to be about the faults or flaws of selected agency employees.
- If you develop a significant problem with a co-worker within the agency, then share this information with your faculty field liaison as soon as possible. Conform to the National Association of Social Workers (NASW) Code of Ethics—do not engage in unethical behavior.
- Keep a positive attitude. Even if the agency does not conform to your ideal image, considerable learning can occur in every practicum. If you have decided (or even if you and your faculty field liaison have decided) that a different placement is necessary next semester, do not

adopt the attitude that you will do just enough to get by. (One worthwhile reason to try your best is that you might want your field instructor to write a good letter of reference for a future job.)

If you truly want to learn and to help the clientele of your agency, then you will almost automatically meet most of the agency's performance standards. By following these guidelines, you are practically guaranteed of meeting all of the agency's expectations and receiving a positive evaluation.

What Do I Do If the Field Instructor Becomes Incapacitated?

Occasionally, events such as accidents, illnesses, or planned absences may mean that your field instructor is unable to continue with your supervision. Your field instructor and faculty field liaison should have sufficient time to make alternative arrangements for planned absences (e.g., vacations). However, your faculty field liaison may not always know when your field instructor is unavailable to supervise you because of unplanned absences such as an accident or illness. In this situation, it is your responsibility to inform your faculty field liaison of such absences—particularly when it is likely that more than one supervisory session will be missed.

IDEAS FOR ENRICHING YOUR PRACTICUM EXPERIENCE

1. What characteristics or features of a social service agency do you think are absolutely essential for it to be a practicum setting for social work students? Jot down your ideas and compare them with the ideas of your fellow students enrolled in the integrating seminar. Alternatively, save your list and examine it at the end of the placement to see if any of your ideas have changed.

2. If you were the supervisor of students in a social service agency, what kinds of attitudes, abilities, and knowledge would you expect them to acquire during their field instruction? How close do these come to the criteria that will be used to evaluate you? Obtain a copy of the evaluation form that your field instructor or faculty field liaison will use and compare.

3. Determine if your social work program keeps students' evaluations of their practicum agencies. If so, read student remarks about the agencies that interest you. Which sound like serious concerns? If your program does not systematically collect evaluations on the practicum settings, determine if there is enough interest to begin gathering this information at the end of each academic term.

4. What agencies are used most often for practicum settings by your social work program? Are different agencies used for undergraduate and graduate field experiences? Is there a good balance in terms of fields of service (e.g., child welfare, mental health, gerontology)?

5. If the curricula vitae for the field instructors used by your social work program are available, then examine several to understand the diversity and richness of their experiences and special expertise. Do you see yourself having a similar curriculum vitae in another 8 to 10 years? What are your career goals?

CASE VIGNETTE TO STIMULATE YOUR THINKING

You have a friend, Heather, in the social work program. Heather always seems to be too busy for her own good. Typically, she runs a day or two late in turning in major assignments. You are aware that she is working full time and trying to go to school full time. You suspect that she is not getting support from her family and may be helping out with expenses at home. It seems that she must be getting only 4 or 5 hours of sleep each night. Still, she is active in several volunteer organizations around town. Heather leads the faculty field liaison to think that she is working only part time on weekends.

Possibly because she failed to note it on her calendar, Heather missed one of the days that she was scheduled to work at her practicum agency. The next time she appeared, her field instructor inquired whether she had been too ill to call in. Heather was momentarily flustered as she tried to recall what she had been doing. Not wanting the field instructor to know that she was really working a full-time job, Heather made up a flimsy excuse.

Heather's field instructor became increasingly alarmed when Heather was late for appointments 2 weeks in a row. Never being especially prompt, Heather also had a problem in turning in required agency paperwork within the deadlines her field instructor gave. On several occasions she was just barely able to meet the deadline for the billing department by staying later after her field instructor had gone home. Unhappy with this, the field instructor asked Heather to avoid working after normal business hours.

Now, at the midterm evaluation, the field instructor is suggesting to the faculty field liaison that Heather be terminated. Heather is confused, hurt, and angry. She has been trying her best, and although she admits to missing a few appointments and deadlines, she really does care for and relate well to the agency's clients. She wants to bring some clients to the midterm evaluation so that they can attest to the good work she has been doing with them.

QUESTIONS

As a field instructor, how would you evaluate Heather?

What do you consider to be her biggest mistake?

Would you give her another chance?

Under what conditions would you decide not to terminate Heather?

Should she plan to bring clients to the midterm evaluation?

REFERENCES

Kadushin, A. (1972). *The social work interview.* New York: Columbia University Press.

National Association of Social Workers. Code of Ethics as adopted by the 1979 NASW Delegate Assembly, effective July 1, 1980.

Suzuki, S. (1970). *Zen mind, beginner's mind.* New York: Weatherhill.

Wilson, S. (1981). *Field instruction: Techniques for supervisors.* New York: Free Press.

ADDITIONAL READINGS

Browstein, C. (1981). Practicum issues: A placement planning model. *Journal of Education for Social Work, 17*(3), 52–58.

Gelman, S. R. (1990). The crafting of fieldwork training agreements. *Journal of Social Work Education, 26*(1), 65–75.

Hepworth, D. H., & Larsen, J. A. (1990). Negotiating goals and formulating a contract. In *Direct social work practice: Theory and skills* (pp. 336–371).

Leader, A. L. (1971). An agency's view toward education for practice. *Journal of Education for Social Work, 7,* 27–34.

Lide, P. D., & Alexander, G. (1975). An educational partnership: Preparing social workers for a changing society. *Journal of Education for Social Work, 11*(1), 94–98.

Rosenfeld, D. J. (1989). Field instructor turnover. In Miriam S. Raskin (Ed.), *Empirical studies in field instruction.* New York: Haworth Press.

Selig, A. L. (1982). Responsibilities of the field instruction agency. In B. W. Sheafor & L. E. Jenkins (Eds.), *Quality field instruction in social work.* White Plains, NY: Longman.

CHAPTER **3**

Getting Started

Overview

Most students want their practicum experiences to be instructive, exciting, and gratifying. But before the practicum can start, the student often must be interviewed in the agency. Even if an interview is not required, the student is likely to be a little nervous about getting off on the right foot and making a good impression. This chapter provides some suggestions for students preparing to go into an agency for the first time.

How Do I Find an Agency That Meets My Needs?

The amount of student input allowed in the choice of a practicum agency varies across social work programs. In some programs, students are permitted to contact agencies and interview them on their own. In programs at the other extreme, students are assigned an agency and have very little choice. Most programs allow students to state preferences or to become actively involved in the selection process. Correspondingly, most agencies want to interview prospective students before agreeing to accept them for a placement.

Even if you are not allowed much leeway in this area, you should consider several important topics as you plan for a practicum. Everyone wants the student to have a positive learning experience. However, occasionally students or agencies will have special requirements and discussing them with your faculty field liaison will result in a better learning experience.

Transportation.   Getting to and from the agency can be a problem for students without a car. Students need to consider where the agency is located in relationship to where they live and go to class. Many agencies are located near college campuses and are easy to reach. Others are some distance away and require ownership of a car, availability of public transportation, or arrangements for car pooling with other students or employees.

If you have a car or access to one, some agencies may ask you to use your car to transport clients or make home visits. Other agencies have cars available for student use. If you are required to drive an agency car, you should speak to your agency supervisor about the extent of insurance coverage to protect you in case of an accident. If you drive your own car, you need to check with your insurance agent about your liability coverage.

Scheduling.   Agencies vary considerably with regard to hours of operation, from those open only a few days per week (this is often the case with new agencies or those that operate almost entirely with volunteers) to those that provide intervention 24 hours per day, 7 days per week.

Some students can be very flexible as they plan their agency time. Others must work around job responsibilities and family commitments and are far less adaptable. Agencies are aware of these differences, and although some are able to accommodate students' schedules, others simply cannot. Students whose schedules are restricted must find agencies that are open at times they can work.

Even if your schedule appears to have no complications (e.g., your classes are on Tuesdays and Thursdays and the agency agrees to accept you as a student on Mondays, Wednesdays, and Fridays), be alert to potential problems such as staff meetings on Tuesday afternoons—a day when you are not scheduled to be in the agency. This circumstance would probably necessitate that you consider a different agency because staff meetings are an important experience in professional socialization. In staff meetings students can observe how the agency operates and how professionals interact with one another. In addition, students can learn what problems are facing the agency and how they will be resolved.

Supervision.   Some students want agency expectations laid out in clear and behaviorally specific terms. They want to know what to do, when to do it, and how to do it. They do not like wondering whether or not they are meeting agency expectations. One student explained,

> Prior to my first day at work, I was surprised to find that I was feeling anxious. My anxiety was based on a fear that there might be little or no structure, that I might have to roam aimlessly, searching for assignments and feeling generally uncomfortable with my new situation.

Other students want a setting in which they can observe for a while, determine what they would like to do, and then begin to use all of their creative and problem-solving capabilities in a task of their choosing.

When selecting an agency, it is important to consider the amount of super-vision you require. The next step is to share this preference with your faculty field liaison. From prior experience with other students, your faculty field liaison will know which agencies allow employees, students, and volunteers the most freedom and which provide greater supervision.

One undergraduate student, who was placed in an unstructured environment with little supervision, arrived at a day-care center for high-risk children and was told that 15 toddlers were in the next room. She was instructed to go and assist in any way she could. Another undergraduate, in a very structured setting, walked into her agency supervisor's office and was given a schedule of training sessions to be held that week for all hospital student interns. She was assigned specific areas of the hospital in which to work, specific tasks to complete, deadlines by which to accomplish the tasks, and a schedule of supervisory conferences. She was told to begin reading hospital policies and logs of former students. Later, she viewed a video on the hospital's history and projected future.

These examples make it easy to envision how problems might develop for students who want a lot of supervision and who do not get it, or who like to work on their own but whose agency supervisors closely observe and direct their activities. It is important to communicate your preference concerning the degree of supervision, or problems may quickly arise and continue throughout the placement.

Agencies vary widely with regard to what they will allow students to do. Some allow immediate one-on-one contact with clients; others do not allow students to have client interaction without supervision until the second semester. One graduate student told a class of undergraduates going into the field for the first time, "Be prepared for the possibility of spending the initial weeks in your agencies doing nothing but observing." She noted that as a 2nd-year graduate student, with 6 years of social work experience and one graduate practicum completed, she was told by her new field instructor that for the 1st month her only assignment was to observe others at work. The 2nd month she could interview clients but only with another social worker present. Finally, at the start of her 3rd month, assuming things went to the supervisor's satisfaction, she could practice alone.

Most agencies are not this stringent in their supervision of students. Some immediately allow students the opportunity to interact one-on-one with clients. This occurs at both the graduate and undergraduate levels. The variation in students' direct contact with clients can be explained by many factors, among them the staff–client ratio, the complexity of the students' tasks, and the con-sequences of students making poor judgments.

Populations, Problem Areas, and Networking. Ideally, students should find placements where they can learn about populations and problem areas that excite them. The agency you select should capture your interests and challenge you to become actively involved. Although it is possible to learn something in any placement, students are most energized when they can immediately immerse themselves in a setting where they easily relate to the primary client group present (e.g., infants, preschoolers, adolescents, elderly) or are curious about the problems with which the agency deals (e.g., chemical dependency, teenage runaways, spouse abuse, juvenile offenders, the terminally ill). Especially before the first placement, students should reflect on what their areas of interest are and which age groups they interact with best.

Some agencies that do more networking, are more interrelated with other agencies, and thus provide a broader practicum experience. Students who want to learn about other social service organizations and the interactions among them should consider how much networking a particular agency does. For example, a family counseling agency that works almost entirely with middle income families may have little cause to work with other agencies in the community. On the other hand, an agency that works with pregnant teens will make connections with social insurance agencies, county or state social service departments, health departments, hospital social service departments, childbirth education organizations, legal services, and residential facilities. Students interested in maximizing their knowledge about other agencies and community resources would receive more of this type of learning in the latter example.

Agency Value Base.   Another area for students to consider is an agency's value base. Once students identify the value base of a potential field agency, they should decide if it creates a conflict with their own. For example, a student who believes that abortion is morally wrong will have a difficult time working in a setting where clients are often referred for abortions. Likewise, a student whose religious ethic is opposed to divorce may have difficulties in a setting where persons are frequently supported for leaving their spouses.

Often our clients' behaviors or values may not be the same as ours. As professionals, we learn to accept individual clients as worthwhile persons although we may not condone their every behavior. Although it is important to know our strongly held values and even to examine them from time to time, it is also worth remembering that values are not permanently fixed. Many people, particularly those acquiring college degrees, are continually updating the facts that form the foundation for their opinions and values. A 19-year-old undergraduate may strongly believe in the death penalty, thinking that certain incarcerated individuals are deserving of this punishment. With this value, that student may not be very successful in some criminal justice placements. However, by the time the same student is in graduate school, he or she may have learned that the poor and minorities have a much greater likelihood of ending up on death row. Seeing the evidence of racism within the legal system, the student may now view the death penalty quite differently and be able to work with inmates on death row.

In the process of obtaining a social work education, students become aware of their own basic values and the values of the profession, and they are challenged to understand the impact of their values on their interactions with others. Personal and professional growth occurs when we examine our values and the stereotypes we hold. However, students should not be forced to act against their basic principles. In such a situation or at any time when you cannot be objective, you should inform your field instructor and discuss transferring or referring the case.

If this poses any problem, a three-way meeting with your faculty field liaison, field instructor, and you should be convened.

How Do I Prepare for the Practicum Interview?

Anticipation of the initial interview with a prospective agency supervisor can produce anxiety. One undergraduate student recalled,

> I phoned the executive director of the agency and arranged for an interview. In the day or two before I was to see her, I unexpectedly discovered that I was feeling quite nervous. Upon examining my feelings, I found that I feared such things as: They won't like me. I won't like them. They will find my dress too casual. I will find them too stuffy. All of these fears could be categorized under a basic "fear of the unknown."
>
> To my surprise, the interview went very well. The director talked about the agency and its purpose and her ideas about students' roles. She asked me about my background and interest in social work and she shared some personal experiences about her own agency work. Before I knew it, an hour had passed. It was a relief to know rapport had definitely been established between us.

Not all first interviews go nearly as well. One student recalled how she was caught totally off guard:

> When I was interviewing for a practicum placement last semester, I was asked what would seem to be a simple question. However, the manner in which the question was asked intimidated me. The interviewer, a stern looking middle-aged clinical social worker, folded her hands, looked me straight in the eye, and asked, "Just yesterday I interviewed another student. Tell me why I should choose you over other students?" I remember frantically trying to think of a good reason. I'm sure my voice was shaking when I asked her to repeat the question (I wanted to stall for time). I ended up giving her two or three reasons, none of which sounded very convincing to me. From then on I was unnerved. When I left the interview, that question was about the only thing I could remember!

Although there is no way to guarantee that your first interview with a potential agency supervisor will be a fun experience, a few steps can be taken to increase the likelihood of a positive experience. Many people find it difficult to speak extemporaneously about their strengths, weaknesses, qualifications, career goals, skills, and abilities. For example, some students may find it difficult to answer the following questions:

- What led you to social work?
- Why do you think you are qualified to be a student intern at this agency?
- How would you describe yourself?
- What talents do you have?
- What do you plan on doing 5 or 10 years from now?

- What can you bring to our agency?
- Why should we consider you as a student intern?
- What problems do you think will be most difficult for you to deal with in this agency setting?

Yet these questions and others may be asked during your interview. Fortunately, it is possible to prepare for questions you may encounter.

Making a detailed self-assessment is one way to prepare for an interview. You should be able to describe traits and skills that contribute to your uniqueness. You might begin by compiling a list of positive adjectives that characterize you (e.g., ambitious, trustworthy, reliable, compassionate, intellectual). Next, narrow the list to three or four items that summarize your personality. You should be able to use examples to illustrate particular attributes (e.g., one undergraduate described himself as "committed" and then explained how he continued working for a summer youth camp during a 3-week period when funding shortages meant he did not receive any pay). Once you have specific attributes and examples in mind, it is fairly easy to respond to the request, "describe yourself."

Trace skills (e.g., the ability to work in stressful situations) to concrete, specific experiences. Describe a particular experience to show how you have used this skill (e.g., you managed an office for 2 weeks by yourself while other office personnel were on leave). In closing your discussion, repeat the skill used. You should be deliberate in describing a strength relative to the position sought (e.g., knowledge of medical terminology when seeking a practicum within a hospital setting). As attorneys do in a courtroom, you want to "build a case"—present "evidence" that you actually possess the traits and skills you say you have.

What Can I Do to De-emphasize Little or No Work Experience?

Both graduate and undergraduate students worry that they will be asked about their lack of practical experience. This anxiety sometimes blocks the memory of past experiences that are related to the demands of the desired practicum. To avoid overlooking relevant experiences, consider your significant past activities before the interview. Perhaps you did volunteer work, were employed in a family business, or were a member of a community service or school organization. Next, make a list of the skills you needed to complete assignments in those settings. You are now ready to link your past with what the current agency needs.

Begin by telling the interviewer what you have done in the past. Next, use a transitional statement to link the past to the present. An undergraduate student gave the following example:

> As leader of my daughter's Girl Scout troop for 2 years, I coordinated group activities for 8- and 9-year-olds. I found I was organized and creative. I think I would be able to build upon this experience when working here in the after-school program.

Even jobs that were not social work related (e.g., working in a pharmacy or supermarket) show that you have learned how to balance schoolwork and other responsibilities, and more likely than not, you picked up valuable skills in working with people.

Is It Wise to Admit My Weaknesses?

In an interview, agency supervisors may ask potential student interns to describe their weaknesses. Questions such as these are asked: What weaknesses do you have? What aspect of this placement do you think will be the most difficult? What is the biggest hindrance you will have to deal with if we select you as a student intern? To prepare for this type of question, consider any potential weaknesses you may have and then rehearse a response using one of the following approaches.

One approach is to accentuate the positive. One student remembered,

> When asked what my weaknesses were relative to the placement, I knew that I did not want to focus on any anticipated problems, so I said that I thought my organization, willingness, and flexibility would enable me to handle any difficulties I might have.

A second approach is to state a weakness and then reframe it into a trait that is positive. One student did this in an interview by saying, "Some people would say that I push myself too hard but I like to think of myself as someone who strives for excellence." As another example of reframing, a student said, "Some people think I do not grasp things quickly enough, but I believe that I spend a lot of time trying to completely understand. I find this often helps me to save time in the long run."

A third way to deal with the subject of weaknesses is to explain how you are working on a particular liability and illustrate specific instances in which you have been encouraged by progress. During a practicum interview, a student explained that she gets very nervous speaking in front of a group. She is working on this by volunteering to make more class presentations and taking a public speaking course. She believes that both of these activities are helping her to overcome problems she had previously experienced speaking in public.

Occasionally, students have questions about whether or not medical diagnoses should be mentioned during an interview at an agency. A student with epilepsy informed his faculty field liaison of this, and together they were able to find a placement where people would know how to respond if the student had a seizure. Had the agency supervisor not known that the student's medical condition was the reason for his reluctance to do certain work (e.g., transporting clients), the supervisor might have thought the student was uncooperative.

If you are presently in counseling for an emotional problem, or have been in the recent past, it may be wise to share this information with the faculty field liaison so that the two of you can decide on the best placement for you. It generally is not advised, for instance, for victims of incest or sexual abuse to begin counseling others with the same problem until progress has been made in their own treatment. Similarly, students from alcoholic families should be pretty far into their own recovery before seeking to work intensively with alcoholic clients. Sharing this type of information with the faculty field liaison does not indicate any "weakness" on your part, but does show maturity and good judgment in dealing with a sometimes painful reality.

How much personal information about students should be shared with agencies is a thorny dilemma for faculty field liaisons. For example, if a student has a criminal record, fails to inform the agency of this, and then violates the law again (either harming clients, putting clients at risk, or causing the agency bad publicity), the issue of liability is raised. On the other hand, disclosing this type of information to agencies will undoubtedly induce some to reject a student not only for a placement, but also perhaps later when that individual may apply for a job. Sharing too much information with an agency may not be in the student's best interest.

In general, students should advise their faculty field liaisons of medical conditions or other situations that could affect their agency work or have repercussions for the agency. The faculty field liaison and the student can then jointly decide whether and to what degree to inform the agency. There are no simple rules on this matter; the advantages and disadvantages of revealing personally sensitive information must be weighed in each individual situation. It is always a delicate issue, but can be handled successfully with adequate advance planning.

Consider the following example of how to inform an agency about these matters:

> A student who was on medication for a bipolar disorder discussed this with her faculty field liaison, and the two of them decided on an agency where she would learn needed skills and also receive supervision from an understanding and perceptive agency supervisor. No exceptional information was given to the agency supervisor ahead of time. The student went through the interview the same as any student would, and she and the agency supervisor developed good rapport during the interview. As the interview was drawing to a close, the agency supervisor announced that he was favorably impressed and informed the student that she could begin a placement with the agency. At that time, the student revealed her medication needs but added that she felt secure this would not present a problem to the agency. The supervisor asked a couple of questions for clarification. The student did not go into a detailed history, but answered factually regarding her behavior when she was acting symptomatically and reassured the supervisor that over the past 18 months she had been functioning well—missing fewer days of work or school than others. The supervisor thanked the student for her honesty and began discussing when the student would be available to start the practicum.

In this example, information was not given ahead of time in order not to bias the supervisor against the student. Since the interview had gone well, the student felt comfortable in disclosing. Had the student felt that the interview was not going well and that it was unlikely that she would be invited to join the agency for a practicum, then the faculty field liaison and the student agreed that disclosure was not necessary.

How Should I Respond to Questions about My Educational Preparation?

In a practicum interview, you may be asked to explain how classroom learning will apply to the particular agency setting. Although you cannot foresee every specific question that might be asked, you can prepare by anticipating related questions and mentally reviewing your educational preparation. The following example shows how a little preparation can give you poise and confidence:

> While a graduate student one of the authors tried to locate a placement that would help refine his counseling skills. He contacted an acquaintance at a local community mental health center and inquired about the possibility of an internship. The acquaintance, the director of the agency, seemed interested and supportive but suggested that the student attend the next "team" meeting at the center and make the request at that time. Not wishing to seem impolite, the student wondered why he would have to make the request a second time but did not seek further explanation. Since he and the director already knew each other from membership in a local organization, the student assumed that the way was smoothed for him to become an intern—only the details would need to be worked out.
>
> On the appointed day, the naive student arrived bright and early but was made to wait outside of the meeting room until "agency business" was concluded. When the meeting ran late, the student began to suspect that team members were arguing about the merits of accepting him as an intern. Finally, after waiting 40 minutes, the student was invited to enter the meeting.
>
> The director made the initial introductions and indicated that the student wanted to become an intern. Then he said, "Tell us something about yourself and your program." The student patiently spoke of his career goals, hobbies, and so on. Somehow this did not seem to be what the team wanted. The student had thought that by now he would be at the end of the interview. However, one of the team members then said, "No, what we want to know is what theoretical approaches do you use when you counsel?" The student's mind raced. Systems theory, reality therapy, Gestalt, and psychoanalysis came to mind. He knew that no one would admit to being Freudian, and he thought about how he would use reality therapy with adolescents. He didn't even know enough about Gestalt to indicate his appreciation of that perspective. Systems theory was not useful in a prescriptive sense. Silently, he hoped for a sudden spark of inspiration. After several false starts, the student said, "I think I'm eclectic."

The point of this illustration is that students should give prior thought to the types of things (e.g., their training or counseling frame of reference) that may interest the interviewer or interviewing staff in the prospective agency.

Interviewers ask questions about educational backgrounds for many reasons. They may be trying to assess intellectual abilities, breadth and depth of knowledge, or special interests or training. To get ready for any questioning along this line, think about your educational experience and then write down two or three courses that were valuable preparation for this specific practicum placement. Next, think of theories or concepts discussed in these courses and write down why you think each would be helpful. This exercise will enable you to go into the interview mindful of important concepts and theories. Interviewers will not expect you to recite an entire course syllabus. However, being able to recall two or three major theories and explain how they relate to the work of the agency would impress many interviewers.

What if the general questions are, "What kind of program do they run there at your university? Is it a good one?" To answer these questions, think about two or three aspects of your social work program that have given you good preparation. For example, some programs incorporate a social work course that requires students to perform a few hours of agency volunteer work each week. This educational experience helps a student know what to expect and what to do in a practicum and could be described as a program strength.

Be positive in describing the valuable learning acquired from your educational experience. An educational program that is described chiefly in negative terms may be seen by some interviewers as inadequately preparing you to function in their agency—as a student or as an employee.

How Should I Dress for the Practicum Agency?

As with many things in life, it is best to avoid extremes. Whether going for the first interview or reporting for work on the 1st day, you should not plan to make a fashion statement. Provocative dress will not be acceptable and may result in losing a placement that you desired. Generally speaking, dress conservatively, but neither too formally nor informally. If possible, visit the agency beforehand and observe what other staff members are wearing. If the staff tends to dress informally (men in sports shirts without ties; women in slacks and casual tops), then dress similarly. If your supervisor and other staff are dressed a little fancier, then use them as models and dress appropriately. Do not wear jeans on the first interview. Later, if you become an intern there and learn that jeans are a fairly standard mode of dress because of the agency population or setting (e.g., assisting clients in a sheltered workshop), then it is usually permissible to wear jeans. When in doubt, dress up a little more than you normally would for going to class.

How Do I Make a Good Impression?

Most initial interviews will last only 30 to 60 minutes. Use this time to make a positive impression by remembering a few simple but important details. First of all, plan to arrive 10 to 15 minutes early. It is always better to be early for an important appointment than to be late. If you plan to arrive early, then even unexpected traffic delays or road construction can be absorbed without causing a major problem.

Second, when you meet the prospective agency supervisor, look the person in the eyes and offer a firm handshake. Smile and show a genuine interest in the person. Take care to pronounce the supervisor's name correctly (if you are unsure, ask). Be prepared to spend the first few minutes making small talk. If you haven't been keeping up with current events, read the local newspaper and a national magazine prior to your meeting. This can help to give you topics for discussion should the conversation move past your credentials. This could easily happen, for example, if your interview was scheduled for 11:00 or 11:15 and the agency supervisor invites you to lunch.

Third, be observant. Look around the office or room and note anything of particular interest to you. One student noticed a guitar sitting in a corner and quickly engaged the supervisor in a discussion about their mutual interest in classical guitar. Meeting strangers is always a little difficult at first. By facilitating conversation with the interviewer, you can demonstrate a skill that will later be required with clients. You will leave a better impression if both you and the interviewer can speak comfortably than if you appear frightened and hesitant to speak.

Fourth, show enthusiasm. One way to do this is to ask questions. Do not be completely passive and think your role is only to wait for questions. Ask questions about the agency, the staff, the clientele, how long the supervisor has been with the agency, and so on. You can ask what formal training is given to students, how student performance is appraised, and what student responsibilities are. Furthermore, you can inquire about what staff you will be working with, the primary functions of the office, and the expected working hours.

Students can usually generate interesting discussion if they have acquired some basic information about the agency prior to the interview, such as

- the relative size of the agency (Has it added or lost staff recently?);
- its organizational auspices (Is it a private or public agency? Where do most of its funds come from?);
- the array of services provided to clients (Who is the "typical" client?); and
- recent news pertaining to the organization (Have there been any recent newspaper articles?).

During the interview, show congruence between your verbal and nonverbal communication. Modulate your voice to maintain the interviewer's attention and be sure to keep appropriate posture. Try to avoid saying what you will not do (e.g., "I will *never* work past 4:30."); rather, emphasize your congeniality and flexibility.

It is wise to keep in mind that many agency supervisors are asking questions in the hopes of answering the following:

- What can you do for the agency?
- How long will it take you to become productive?
- What do you want from the agency?
- Can you handle stress?
- Can you get along with others?

By anticipating questions that interviewers are likely to ask and by knowing the "hidden agenda," there is a greater probability that you will leave a good impression than if you go unprepared.

A day or two after your interview, it would be a nice touch to drop the potential field instructor a brief thank-you note in the mail expressing appreciation for interviewing you. If you schedule three or four interviews, and each agency offers you the opportunity to come there and be an intern, it is always expected that you will call as soon as you have made a decision and inform the other agencies. They may be waiting to hear from you before committing to any other students. Once again, thank them for their interest and assistance.

What Can I Expect on the First Day of a New Practicum?

Agencies prepare for and use students in enormously different ways. Two accounts illustrate this, the first reported by one of the authors:

> The first day in one of my graduate practicums another student and I were handed a scrapbook of clippings about the agency and instructed to familiarize ourselves with the agency's range of activities. We carefully poured over the scrapbook and about 45 minutes later returned it to our supervisor and asked what we should do next. With a look of surprise he informed us that he thought the activity would have taken us most of the day. He actually had made no other plans for us on the 1st day, and said that we could go home. Looking back on this experience now, I realize that very little planning had gone on prior to our arrival.

Another student experienced something quite different:

> I participated in a training session aimed at familiarizing new students with various facets of the agency. The director, co-director, two experienced volunteers, and one agency worker conducted the seminar. Several topics related to agency operations were discussed, such as the importance of confidentiality, agency policies, forms, and procedures.

The atmosphere created by the staff in the latter example enabled the student to feel comfortable about making comments and asking questions. A large part of the training was devoted to role playing by the staff. They acted out several typical cases, demonstrating a variety of likely occurrences. In summary the student commented,

> At the end of the session, we were given the opportunity to assess the worth of the training. I offered my positive comments and left the meeting feeling I had been treated with respect, appreciation, and a genuine concern. The staff seemed to provide me with the knowledge necessary for a productive learning experience.

These examples illustrate differences in orientation. Ideally, the 1st day and perhaps the 1st week should be closer to the second example. Your orientation should include an introduction to the agency (e.g., its mission and services), the staff, and the physical layout of the facility, and an explanation of pertinent agency policies and procedures. However, the planned orientation might have to be abbreviated because agency staff members often take on the supervision of a student intern in addition to their regular responsibilities. They can be pulled away to take care of client emergencies or to attend to other crises within an agency. Occasionally, agency supervisors simply do not have the time to plan activities that will meaningfully or fully involve students on their first day.

On the other hand, some supervisors anticipate from the beginning the ways a student can gain new perspectives and insights into the social work profession while helping with the work that needs to be done. And although it is not uncommon for "disasters" to occur from lack of planning during a student's initial orientation to an agency, settings where there is too little planning, insufficient supervision, and too much chaos do not provide students with the necessary structure. If these terms characterize your placement, you should address this problem by speaking with your faculty field liaison.

How Do I Develop a Learning Contract?

You will probably be given the opportunity to develop contracts with clients in your practicum. To become familiar with the use of contracts, most social work programs will expect you to prepare a learning (or educational) contract of your own—one that outlines your responsibilities in the practicum. This three-way agreement usually involves you, the field instructor, and the faculty field liaison and generally states what you hope to learn from the practicum (i.e., your goals), the responsibilities or tasks that will be given to you, and miscellaneous details such as the amount or extent of supervision you will receive and the hours or days that you will be in the practicum agency. Usually, the three parties will sign and receive a copy of the contract.

The learning contract minimizes the possibility of misunderstandings and provides a basis for accountability. It helps students to keep in mind what they have committed themselves to, provides a sense of progress and satisfaction as portions of it are completed, and helps students to plan their time in the agency (Hamilton & Else, 1983). The learning contract supplies necessary safeguards to insure the integrity of the practicum as an educational experience and to discourage the use of students as substitute employees.

Start working on the learning contract by familiarizing yourself with the practicum requirements of your program and the agency's expectations of you. (Sometimes, all of the students in a given agency are expected to meet certain learning goals, and these may already be stated for you.) Read the practicum syllabus or manual. For example, how many days or hours are you expected to be in the agency each week? Compare your learning needs and career goals with the educational opportunities that will be afforded to you in this placement. Then, draft a set of goals and objectives that you hope to achieve in this practicum.

Note that a distinction has been made between goals and objectives. *Goals* provide a general sense of direction—the target for which you are aiming. *Objectives* are always expressed so that it is easy to monitor whether or not they were accomplished. (It is helpful to use action verbs, to specify a time or date within the objective, and when possible, to identify quantities.) With the help of your field instructor, make sure that your learning objectives are measurable and attainable. For learning goals, think of each active step, activity, or responsibility that you will have to undertake or perform. These will suggest to you the objectives that should fall under each learning goal. Of these tasks or activities, choose the ones that are most directly observable and whose feedback will be essential to your field education. For each objective ask, "How will my field instructor know that I have achieved this objective?"

Identify three or four goals in terms of particular skills or knowledge that you would like to acquire and try to come up with suitable objectives for each. Each achieved objective should help your field instructor know that you have made progress toward reaching a goal. If it will be difficult or impossible to know when you have completed an objective, then the objective is not useful and needs to be rewritten in more behavioral terms. Finally, consider how much time it will take to achieve the objective. If it will take more time than is available to you, then it needs to be discarded. You should have a mixture of a few objectives that can be met within the first several weeks of the practicum, and others that will not be completed until the last several weeks.

When you are reasonably satisfied with the rough draft of your learning contract, share it with your field instructor, and the two of you can then make any necessary revisions. After incorporating the revisions and retyping the document, you may be ready for signatures. However, ask whether or not your faculty field liaison wants to review the contract before obtaining the signature of the field instructor. It is probably best if you don't think of the contract as being in its final form until it has been reviewed by both the field instructor and the faculty field liaison. When there are no further revisions, you and the field agency and school representatives will sign the learning contract. Each of these parties should then receive a copy of the agreement.

There is no single best approach to contract development. However, the SPIRO model (Pfeiffer & Jones, 1972) provides a good set of guidelines that emphasize the following critical characteristics of a contract: *specificity, performance, involvement, realism,* and *observability.*

Specificity demands that your learning goals are specific rather than too general or global. For instance, "To learn how to be a better social worker" is much too general, as is, "To learn how to respond to clients in a professional manner." An evaluation of what the student should be learning at any point in the academic term is facilitated by the more specific goal: "To learn how to screen clients for substance abuse."

By making your learning goals *performance* oriented, all three parties should have a good idea of the activities, duties, assignments, or responsibilities to be completed for you to meet your goals. For instance, it will be necessary to conduct substance abuse screenings in order to learn how to do them. Once the goal has been stated, it is desirable for objectives or tasks to be specified. For instance, a student who wants to learn how to conduct substance abuse screenings might list below that goal the following objective: "To conduct at least ten substance abuse screenings during the practicum placement."

Involvement insures that the contract spells out the extent to which you, the field instructor, and the faculty field liaison will be involved in helping you to reach your learning goals. Obviously, if the field instructor and faculty field liaison approve of this goal, then you will have to be assigned a sufficient number of clients for the goal to be achieved. Your learning contract might specify either that the faculty field liaison will make an evaluative visit to the agency or that you will receive a minimum of 1 hour per week supervision from your field instructor. (This makes the contract more than just a one-sided agreement.)

The element of *realism* is a reminder that your learning goals and associated objectives need to be realistic and attainable within the limits of the agency's educational resources, the time you will be in the practicum, and your personal assets and limitations.

Observability "demands that results be defined in a measurable form so that it is obvious whether or not the specific goal has been achieved" (Abbott, 1986, p. 61). Although the absolute number of substance abuse screenings to be completed may not always be critical, it is important that an impartial observer be able to determine whether or not you have completed your objectives.

Try to strike a balance between ambitiousness and practicality in your learning contract. Discussion with your field instructor and faculty field liaison will help to identify areas where change or modification is needed. A brief example of a learning contract is provided in Figure 3.1 to guide you in your efforts.

IDEAS FOR ENRICHING YOUR PRACTICUM EXPERIENCE

1. Why was your agency originally created or funded? What was its mission statement at its earliest beginning? Has the agency's mission changed over the years? Try to find a copy of the agency's constitution, bylaws, or charter to read.

2. How well known is your agency? How often has your agency or its staff received newspaper coverage in the past year? Ask 10 of your friends, neighbors, or relatives what they know about the agency where you will be placed. If the agency has a unique logo or emblem, how many of the 10 recognize it? How many know where the agency is located? If you feel that the agency does not have a high level of community recognition (based on your small sample), what could be done to make it more visible?

3. Determine whether or not a community resource or referral list is commonly used in your agency. If so, where is it located? When was it updated last? Is it obviously incomplete? Whose responsibility is it to keep the list current? If the list is in serious need of updating and you have the time, ask your field instructor if you can assist with this project.

4. Putting aside your learning contract for a moment, what skills will your current practicum offer you a chance to develop that will interest future employers? How would you describe these skills on a resume or curriculum vitae? (If you do not feel that your practicum is providing you with any marketable skills, you need to discuss ways of enhancing this practicum with your faculty field liaison.)

GEORGE GOODSTUDENT

Placement Agency: Rogers County Mental Health Services
Address: 1414 Evans Drive, Zanesville, Ohio
Phone: (513) 555-5000
Field Instructor: Mary Ann Mobbie, M.S.W.
Hours in Placement: Tuesday: 8:00 A.M. to 5:00 P.M.   Friday: 8:00 A.M. to 5:00 P.M.
Supervision Time: Tuesday: 8:30 A.M. to 10:00 A.M.

GOAL 1: TO IMPROVE INTERVIEWING SKILLS.

Objective 1: To read Cormier's[1] book on interviewing during the 1st week (not on practicum time) and discuss any questions with the field instructor.

Objective 2: To observe five interviews conducted by agency staff by the 2nd week.

Objective 3: To videotape two interviews with clients by the end of the semester.

Objective 4: To conduct at least 12 interviews with clients by the end of the semester.

GOAL 2: TO LEARN THE COMMUNITY'S SOCIAL SERVICES.

Objective 1: By midsemester to visit United Way's Information and Referral Center and interview two staff members about services available.

Objective 2: To read 20 recently closed cases by the 7th week to identify referrals that were made.

Objective 3: To attend at least five case conferences by the end of the semester.

GOAL 3: TO LEARN HOW TO CONDUCT GROUP THERAPY.

Objective 1: To observe for 3 weeks the incest survivors' support group.

Objective 2: To attend the scheduled 4 hour in-service entitled "Working with Groups"

Objective 3: To cofacilitate a new time-limited support group for male sexual abuse victims (8 weeks).

Student _____ Date _____

Field Instructor _____ Date _____

Faculty Field Liaison _____ Date _____

FIGURE 3.1   Sample Practicum Learning Contract

[1] W. H. Cormier. (1985). *Interviewing strategies for helpers: Fundamental skills and cognitive behavioral interventions.* Pacific Grove, CA: Brooks/Cole.

CASE VIGNETTE TO STIMULATE YOUR THINKING

A fellow student in one of your classes begins to share some personal material with you. She was a victim of severe child abuse and reared by foster parents. Although she has never received any individual counseling, she now wants to do a practicum that will place her on a treatment team for children who have been sexually abused. Previously, other students who have completed a practicum with this agency have told you how intense and stressful their placement was. The student who wants to go to this agency hints that such a field experience will be "therapeutic" for her.

QUESTIONS

Do you think her plan for a practicum is a good one?

Would you advise her to choose a different practicum?

On what might your decision depend?

Would it be a good idea for her to inform her field instructor and faculty field liaison of her prior history?

REFERENCES

Abbott, A. A. (1986). The field placement contract: Its use in maintaining comparability between employment-related and traditional field placements. *Journal of Social Work Education, 22*(1), 57–66.

Cormier, W. H. (1985). *Interviewing strategies for helpers: Fundamental skills and cognitive behavioral interventions.* Pacific Grove, CA: Brooks/Cole.

Hamilton, N., & Else, J. (1983). *Designing field education: Philosophy, structure, and process.* Springfield, IL: Charles C. Thomas.

Pfeiffer, J. W., & Jones, J. E. (1972). Criteria of effective goal-setting: The SPIRO model. In *The 1972 annual handbook for group facilitators.* La Jolla, CA: University Associates.

ADDITIONAL READINGS

Bolles, R. N. (1987). *What color is your parachute: A practical manual for job hunters and career changers.* Berkeley, CA: Ten Speed Press.

Dunkel, J., & Hatfield, S. (1986). Countertransference issues in working with persons with AIDS. *Social Work, 31*(2), 114–117.

Golden, N. (1986). *Dress right for business.* New York: Gregg Division, McGraw-Hill Book Co.

Maluccio, A., & Marlow, W. D. (1974). The case for the contract. *Social Work, 19*(1), 28–36.

Peabody, S. A., & Gelso, C. J. (1982). Countertransference and empathy: The complex relationship between two divergent concepts in counseling. *Journal of Counseling Psychology, 29*(3), 240–245.

Pincus, A., & Minahan, A. (1973). Negotiating contracts. In *Social work practice: Model and method* (pp. 162–193). Itasca, IL: F. E. Peacock.

Rodgers, E. J. (1982). *Getting hired: Everything you need to know about resumes, interviews, and job-hunting strategies.* Englewood Cliffs, NJ: Prentice-Hall.

Seabury, B. (1976). The contract: Uses, abuses, and limitations. *Social Work, 21*(1), 16–21.

CHAPTER **4**

The Student Intern: Learning New Roles

Overview

Student interns may feel that they are a hybrid creation—treated sometimes like an employee, sometimes like a volunteer. It is easy to be confused about roles when one is sometimes allowed only to observe professional staff in action, and other times given enormous responsibilities. This chapter attempts to help the student understand the differences between volunteer, student, and employee roles.

What Are the Differences between Volunteer, Student, and Employee Roles?

Every day, each of us is involved in many different roles. For instance, our behavior may reflect our status as a son or daughter, mother or father, student, employee, or volunteer. Social service agencies may differ in how they view student interns, and their understanding of the internship role will determine what students will be given to do, the amount of supervision they will receive, and how their performance will be evaluated. Your own educational experience will be enriched by a clear understanding of the differences between the volunteer, student, and employee roles.

Depending on the agency, the differences between a volunteer and a student intern may be barely perceptible. For instance, both volunteer counselors and student interns at a rape crisis center may have to complete 40 hours of training and orientation before they have any client contact. In other settings, such as a psychiatric unit of a hospital, volunteers (e.g., candy stripers) have very different responsibilities than student interns.

Although students and volunteers might at times be given similar tasks, students have the additional responsibility of learning why a task was done, why it was done the way it was, and how that task relates to the larger picture of planned intervention with a client. Being a student involves thinking, analyzing, and critiquing, as well as doing. Students are expected to see the connection between intervention and overarching theoretical structures. Students should feel that they may ask questions and ask for reference material in areas where they have little knowledge, and should be given the opportunity to observe and practice new skills.

Volunteers tend to be given mundane chores (e.g., addressing envelopes or answering the telephone) because they are seen as just "helping out." Such volunteer assignments generally do not require close supervision. Although you as a student may be given some of the same responsibilities as volunteers, these should make up only a small portion of your time in the practicum. If you find that the bulk of your practicum time is filled with tedious chores that do not allow you to grow intellectually as a social worker, then it may be that your agency views you more as a volunteer than as a student.

As a student, you ought to be working with clients directly (unless you are in certain administrative or research placements) in such a way that necessitates at least an hour or two of weekly supervision. Ask your field instructor questions and keep him or her current on the progress of your cases. The supervision should not be limited to an evaluation of how well you performed a task, but should also include suggestions from the field instructor regarding other approaches, strategies, and theories, or the sharing of how the field instructor handled a similar case (more on how to make the best use of supervision later in this chapter).

Unlike volunteers who may work as much or little as pleases them, students have a specified number of practicum hours that must be spent in their assigned agencies. Both volunteers and students need their supervisors to agree to their proposed schedules before starting in the agency. Sometimes days and hours are negotiated—one day might be more convenient than another. This contrasts rather markedly with the employee who is told what days and exact hours to work. Employees may be given little choice in tasks or responsibilities to perform. Agencies expect more from employees than from students or volunteers in terms of productivity and knowledge about their jobs. But then, of course, employees are generally rewarded financially for their trials and tribulations.

In some situations, clients accept volunteers more easily than they do students. One undergraduate volunteering in a mental hospital explained,

> The patients were more accepting of me when I was a volunteer because they believed I came to the hospital not because of a course requirement, but because I cared and wanted to be with them. They saw students as being interested in them as subjects for research rather than as individual human beings.

Students placed in residential facilities may find that residents resent students who come into their lives and then leave abruptly at the end of the academic term.

Unlike employees and students, volunteers are seldom evaluated. Generally speaking, there are never enough volunteers in agencies, and even inept volunteers are often tolerated. Volunteers are informed that their services are no longer needed if they are unreliable (e.g., they don't show up on the days expected or don't accomplish assigned tasks) or obnoxious. Students, on the other hand, are usually formally evaluated at the midpoint and toward the end of their academic terms. Social work students' experience in the practicum is guided (and to some degree regulated) by their learning contracts, which specify educational goals and objectives. Faculty field liaisons insure that meaningful learning is occurring and help troubleshoot any problems that may develop.

Students sometimes suspect that they are being treated not as students or staff but as free labor. For instance, one student complained bitterly when she was asked (in a residential setting) to help with some of the housekeeping chores. However, all of the paid staff were expected to perform certain menial chores to keep the facility clean and neat. The student was not being asked to do anything that staff members themselves did not do. This is not an unreasonable expectation. However, students should be concerned when the majority of assignments seem to be more related to housekeeping than to professional responsibilities. If you think that you are being unjustly treated just because you are a student, then you have a legitimate complaint that you should share with your field instructor. On the other hand, if you are being assigned what you consider an unpleasant chore or responsibility that other staff members also perform or take turns doing, then you probably have little reason to complain (but you may now see the importance of having a very specific learning contract).

Do Students Have the Same Privileges as Staff Members?

You may be abruptly reminded that you are a student, not an employee, when you arrive at the agency extra early some morning and find the doors locked. You might not get in because you don't have a key. Similarly, you may not be able to work late because you can't lock up. Although being an employee of an agency implies certain responsibilities, usually there are other perks that also go along.

For instance, the agency may recognize a holiday that your university doesn't. The employees will get that day off, but if it falls on a day that you are scheduled to be in the agency, you will have to make up that time. You may find that the secretary in the agency treats the work you ask to be typed with a lower priority than she does that of the regular employees.

Even though in other areas you feel like a part of the team, you may be caught off guard when an incident suddenly reminds you of your internship status. This might happen when a long-time employee is retiring and a group of employees decides to take this person to lunch. You might be asked to stay behind and answer the phones in their absence. Or your field instructor may not inform you about a planned agency-wide retreat or special staff meeting.

These minor affronts should be ignored, for the most part. It is helpful to remember that your role is of a student and others in the agency may have privileges that you don't. This doesn't mean that they dislike you, but it could mean that they view you as a transient. In fact, you are there only temporarily.

If, however, you feel that you have a contribution to make at the special staff meeting, or that attending the planned retreat can be justified educationally, then inform your field instructor that you would like to attend and ask if it would be appropriate for you to do so.

What Do I Need to Know about Interdisciplinary Team Meetings?

Many students will have the opportunity to participate on interdisciplinary teams and attend their meetings. As a rule, the initial student role is of observer until the student has a case to present or is asked to become more involved by the field instructor or other team member. This will usually happen after the student has had occasion to work with or observe clients being discussed by the team.

Interdisciplinary teams are made up of people, each of whom possesses particular expertise and is responsible for individual decisions and actions. Team members share a common purpose as they meet together to pool knowledge, ideas, and plans for intervention. Interdisciplinary teams offer a framework within which specialists can work together to provide services for the total life experience of a client (Brill, 1990). Teams are often found in institutions such as nursing homes, schools, hospitals, rehabilitation centers, and prisons.

Students need to understand the overall purpose of a particular team, who makes up the team, how membership is decided, and its agreed goals. The goals determine how often the team will meet and how it will reach and implement decisions. It is also helpful to know the backgrounds of the individual team members, who operate out of their own philosophies, roles, and attitudes. Each person's unique perspective allows for consideration of the problem from many different angles. These points of view justify each person's inclusion on the team.

If you are expected to be an active team member rather than an observer, do not be intimidated. You may have information not acquired by other professionals, or a better relationship with the client that has allowed new information to sift out. Especially if you have had an opportunity to see the client in a different capacity (e.g., to observe interaction with other clients or with family members), your insights will be valued.

When you are not speaking, listen carefully to what each person is saying. Come prepared and be familiar with the cases that are to be discussed. As a social worker, facilitate communication, provide information useful for problem solving, and see that arrangements are made for any needed coordination of services.

How Much Will I Be Given to Do?

The amount of work assigned to students in practicum varies greatly. Students who possess more maturity, intelligence, competence, and prior experience will probably end up with larger caseloads than students who lack one or more of these traits. At least one crisis counseling agency requires that every student spend the first semester observing and listening to the way their counselors handle emergency calls before being given the responsibility of staffing the crisis phone lines in the second semester. If a student plans to intern for two consecutive academic terms in that agency, then it is very likely there will be a smaller caseload in the first term than in the second.

In most agencies, a rough rule of thumb is that student interns might expect to carry four to seven cases at a time. Two or three cases are too few and ten or more are often too many unless a student is in a block placement and working 30 hours or more a week in the agency. Four or five cases will keep a student reasonably occupied—especially if these have different diagnoses or distinctive problems that require background or additional reading.

It is true that four or five cases will not keep a student completely occupied if he or she is placed in an agency for 20 hours per week or so. At a minimum, students might expect to be involved in some type of professional activity at least half of the time. In addition to managing their own cases, students often can assist with intake evaluations, participate in case conferences or staff meetings, accompany other staff who make home visits, and observe group or family therapy sessions. By planning ahead, students might ask to participate in a particular type of session (e.g., termination with a client) that they will need to handle by themselves later in the academic term.

Since agencies vary markedly with regard to their clientele, some students may find that they have few clients, but these are ongoing or long term; while students in other agencies may have many more clients over the academic term, but these tend to involve briefer contacts. Actually, a combination of both short- and long-term clients would be ideal. Optimally, a student should receive clients at intake and keep them throughout the treatment process until the clients terminate services.

As a student, it is to your advantage to learn as much as possible about the agency and the way it serves its clientele. If you feel that you are being under-utilized, talk with your field instructor. He or she may agree to your taking on other assignments within the agency. Perhaps you could assist with a small research or evaluation project. It may be possible, for instance, to contact previous clients to determine if they require additional intervention from the agency. You could plan this sort of project whenever things are reasonably caught up and in between other scheduled clients or activities.

Another useful educational strategy is to interview staff with whom you do not have the opportunity to work. Ask them what they think is important to know in order to do their jobs well. Be assertive in meeting other staff members as you attempt to get more involved in the agency. If after these efforts you still feel that too much of your time is being wasted, then it is appropriate to inform your faculty field liaison. Problems you encounter during your field instruction are the mutual responsibility of three parties: the faculty field liaison, the field instructor, and you. All three must be involved to ensure the integrity of the field instruction.

What Happens If I Make a Mistake?

It is hard to go through life (or maybe even a week) without making some kind of a small mistake. What happens if you make a small mistake in your practicum? First, let's examine what might be considered a small mistake: You have promised a client that you would obtain information about a community resource and you forgot to do so. After an interview with a client, you remember an important question you had intended to ask. You fail to get a client's signature on a necessary form. These problems are not serious because each can be easily resolved by a phone call or at the time of the client's next visit.

Some mistakes are more serious than these. For example, you might inadvertently disclose confidential information about a client receiving services to someone whom the client did not want to know. In instances where you have done something that could lead a client to file a complaint with the agency, you should inform your field instructor as soon as possible.

Minor mistakes may cause some inconvenience (e.g., a client having to make another trip to the agency to sign a form), but major mistakes violate rights or have the potential to cause harm. Always inform your field instructor about major mistakes, but it is not necessary to mention every little oversight. When in doubt, it is better to inform your field instructor than to treat the mistake as a secret.

How Much Will I Be Supervised, and by Whom?

A qualified social work supervisor (field instructor) should be regularly accessible within the agency where you are placed. If your immediate agency supervisor does not hold a social work degree, then another person with social work credentials may be asked to provide your formal or official supervision at least once a week. In a few instances where a program or agency does not employ any social workers but where a rich learning opportunity is available, a social work faculty member may be asked to provide your supervision.

Your agency supervisor will be responsible for giving you duties or assignments and monitoring your performance. He or she will be in charge of you, and unless you are informed to the contrary, this is the person to whom you should turn if you have any questions or problems while carrying out your assignments.

A major difference between the type of supervision you will receive as a student and other nonprofessional supervision that you may have experienced in paid employment or voluntary jobs is that the field instructor has a major teaching role. Field instructors attempt to introduce students to a wide range of activities performed by social workers. In keeping with their teaching role, they may also assign readings to assist students in better understanding their clients or improving certain skills. Practicum experience is designed to help students learn specific social work skills and knowledge in accordance with their learning contracts.

Field instructors and agencies vary with respect to the amount of individual supervision they give students. Until you demonstrate that you can handle certain tasks, you may feel that your supervisor is monitoring very closely (looking over your shoulder). Gradually, as you demonstrate your competence and the two of you get to know each other a little more, supervision may become more relaxed.

From an agency's perspective, students require supervision (sometimes very close supervision), which takes away from the field instructor's own productivity—unless the students contribute in such a way as to offset the investment of time. Students who require too much supervision and who cannot be trusted with even the most menial of assignments will cause the agency to expend more resources on the student than will be returned.

Most often, field instructors will be cautious not to give students any assignments that would exceed their level of expertise. The initial tasks may be fairly elementary. Agency supervisors will gauge students' performance on these tasks before giving them more advanced or demanding assignments. If your work is sloppy and careless, there will be little reason to give you more responsibility or more complex assignments. Similarly, if you take too long or fail to complete your assignments, you will not be perceived as a resource or an asset to the agency but rather as a liability.

In our experience, the amount of time allotted for supervisory conferences changes as the semester progresses. Generally, supervisors spend more time with students at the beginning of the placement than once students are past the first several weeks of orientation. Field instructors want to get students off to a good start and want to be sure that students understand agency policy and procedure. Once students are involved and doing well, supervisors may not be so deliberate or constant in monitoring how they are doing.

Because students seem to do better when supervision is consistent and predictable, we recommend that you set a specific time each week with the field instructor to ensure that supervision occurs. If this detail was overlooked in your learning contract, do not let several weeks go by without at least one hour of supervision. Do not settle for 5 minutes here and 10 minutes there. The quality of supervision provided on the run is not the same as when both of you have time to think about what you have been learning and what you still need to learn.

How Do I Make Supervision Work for Me?

Getting the most out of supervision requires that you know what supervision is, what the dynamics of the supervisory relationship are, and what specific actions facilitate effective supervision.

Supervisors oversee the work of others. Supervisors administer and coordinate; they provide consultation to help those whom they supervise perform more effectively and efficiently. Supervisors explain important agency policies and procedures, provide on-the-job training, assess performance, and make suggestions for improvement. In addition, supervisors participate in the hiring and firing of employees, mediate problems between their subordinates and the agency, and sometimes fill in for employees who are sick or absent. They are depositories of knowledge about the agency and the clientele. Above all else, supervisors are responsible for seeing that clients are provided quality services.

Interesting dynamics are generated in the process of supervision. From the subordinate's perspective, some supervisors are not good teachers or leaders. They may not know how to correct gently or how to make a suggestion without it sounding like criticism. Unfortunately, these supervisors can hurt feelings without intending to do so. A former student once reported that her supervisor thought that she "had to be critical" or else the student wouldn't think that she had a knowledgeable field instructor.

From the supervisor's perspective, there are individuals who resent having a boss or someone who is "over" them and who can tell them what to do. Supervisors have a difficult time overseeing individuals who are irritated at the very thought of having to account for their activities and who may find passive-aggressive ways to sabotage a supervisory relationship (e.g., showing up late for supervision, or "forgetting" about a supervisory conference and scheduling a client at the same time).

Sometimes mature or nontraditional social work students have had managerial experience in other careers before deciding to become social workers. It may be difficult in such situations to accept the fact that, although they may be peers in age or in other life experiences, the subordinate–supervisor relationship is not a peer or reciprocal relationship.

The time that you spend with your agency supervisor should be an opportunity for you to grow professionally, by availing yourself of the supervisor's greater store of practice experience and knowledge. If you are feeling overwhelmed or confused, supervisors can help you to rank your tasks so that the most important ones are completed first. If you do not know how to do your assigned jobs, your supervisor can provide direction as to what to do, how to do it, and when.

A good supervisor should reduce your anxiety and increase your sense of competence and self-worth by listening to you and being concerned when you have problems. He or she should be a successful problem solver who follows through with commitments. Hopefully, your supervisor will be someone who tells you what you are doing that is correct, so that you can keep doing it, and explains what you are doing that is unacceptable, so that you can rectify it (Egan, 1990).

You can get the most out of your supervisory conferences by planning for them. Before a scheduled conference, write down a list of questions you have, problems you want to discuss, or observations that you want to make. Be prepared to inform your agency supervisor what assignments you have accomplished and which are nearing completion. Be able to account for how you have spent your time. If you are not being given enough to do, ask for new assignments or additional responsibilities.

If you have a client who is making no progress or who is a difficult case, then take advantage of the time with your agency supervisor to discuss it. There may be other ways to view the problem, or alternative treatment strategies or resources—or the case may be too complex for a student to handle. We all learn from our mistakes. Do not be afraid to be completely honest with your agency supervisor. For instance, assume that you unthinkingly used a poor choice of words, which seemed to offend Mrs. Jones. She stormed off in anger. You feel that it is your fault and that the client may never return to the agency. By sharing this with your supervisor, you may learn that Mrs. Jones is irascible and in the past has stomped off in anger on the average of once a month or so. Instead of being worried (and maybe guilty) about offending Mrs. Jones, sharing this information may help you to learn more about Mrs. Jones' personality and level of functioning.

Supervision can help you to develop professionally—but only if you want to learn from it. Ask questions about things you want to know. Ask for articles or books that would help you to understand the cases you are handling. Be active in learning from your supervisor. Reflect on the feedback you have been given. Make your role as a subordinate work to your advantage.

What Is the Purpose of Field Seminars?

As a part of the practicum requirements, many social work programs require students to participate in weekly seminars. A *seminar* is a small group of students engaged in a special study under the guidance of a professor. Scheduled meetings are held for the exchange of ideas around a particular topic. The basic assumption underpinning seminars is that each person in attendance has important information to share or contribute. By contrast, in lecture courses the assumption is that the professor has the most knowledge and will be the prime communicator of ideas.

Usually, field seminars are conducted by faculty field liaisons, although they may be directed by field instructors or even students themselves. Faculty field liaisons or seminar leaders make arrangements for the time and place of the meeting, and determine the frequency of the seminars as well as the focus of each session. In addition, it is their responsibility to see that the discussions are relevant to students' current experiences in their practicum placements. Many see their seminar leadership role as helping students (1) to understand their cases in terms of applicable theories, and (2) to integrate discoveries in an area (e.g., practice) with content from another (e.g., policy or research implications).

Seminars may be highly structured, as when students are given specific reading assignments or asked to make presentations. Or, seminars may be loosely structured, as when students may each take a turn relating significant experiences or problems that recently occurred in the field. In structured seminars, it is likely that the faculty field liaison will choose the topics and carefully focus student discussion. Similarly, the faculty field liaison may give specific directions for seminar presentations. Here are a few suggestions if you are required to make a presentation:

1. Keep within the time limit (organize your thoughts and rehearse your presentation).
2. Begin with a brief introduction of what you intend to cover.
3. Limit your main points to three or four and support these with illustrations.
4. Summarize your main points at the end of your presentation.
5. Stimulate discussion by looking at each person as you speak.
6. Use visual aids to clarify ideas.
7. Anticipate questions, and to encourage discussion, ask several questions of your own.

Whether they are structured or unstructured, most faculty field liaisons prefer that all students contribute to seminar discussions. Informal exchanges can help to increase comfort with a client's diagnosis, or the way intervention is proceeding. Learning that your peers have had similar experiences or even that they would have handled the problem the same way you did can be very reassuring. In the best seminars, students can feel free to raise questions of the faculty member or other students—to ask for resources or help with a special situation or problem.

To get the most out of an unstructured seminar, prepare ahead of time by reflecting on the past week's important events. Rank order these when time is limited so that the most pressing matters can be discussed first. Try not to monopolize the group's time. In some instances, it may be necessary to continue the discussion with your faculty field liaison after the seminar or to make an appointment for this purpose.

In seminars, you are expected to be a good listener when others are speaking, to stay alert, and to interact with others in the group. A seminar works well only when everyone takes part of the responsibility to make it interesting by raising questions and sharing information that may not be common knowledge.

How Will My Faculty Field Liaison Evaluate Me?

There is no way we can inform you of exactly what your faculty field liaison will personally expect of you. However, you can get some idea of these expectations from the syllabus and from the instructor's presentation at the first class meeting (or at the time you received your syllabus or field manual). This is the time to ask questions if you specifically want to know more about how you will be evaluated.

However, on the basis of our own experiences supervising students in the field and our contacts with other faculty field liaisons, it is possible for us to talk very generally about what faculty field liaisons expect of students. To understand this perspective, you must keep in mind that although faculty field liaisons are concerned with what you are learning and your performance in the agency, they are at the disadvantage of not seeing very much (if any) of your work in the agency. Because they have the responsibility of assigning a grade to your efforts, they need feedback from your agency supervisor and possibly such evidence as they can collect from assignments. Some faculty field liaisons allow written assignments to carry more weight than feedback and evaluations from agency supervisors. These faculty field liaisons typically expect that all assignments will be completed no later than the date due, that any field logs or process recordings will be kept current, and that you show up for scheduled appointments to discuss the placement. If your grade is more dependent on written assignments than on agency input, then you may earn a lower grade than you think you deserve, even if you are doing superior work in the agency.

Grading schemes are often somewhat subjective. One faculty field liaison may let the course grade be largely determined by the agency supervisor's recommendation; another may weigh more heavily written assignments or case presentations; a third may penalize you for missing seminars or classes; and a fourth may pass everyone as long as no problems occurred in the agency. Your course syllabus should state specifically how your grade will be determined. Many programs use a pass/fail method, which seems to take pressure off grades.

You can avoid failing or unsatisfactory grades, as a rule, by following the syllabus and using common sense. Beyond this, conventional wisdom would tell you to avoid asking for exceptions to existing policy or rules. The following true illustrations are provided to help you understand what faculty field liaisons *do not* want in their students. One student, who decided about halfway through the semester that she didn't like her practicum, went into the agency on a Sunday morning and, without telling anyone, cleaned out her desk. Later, she informed her university instructor of what she had done. (A more responsible student would have informed the faculty field liaison of perceived problems in the agency and would have allowed the faculty field liaison time to investigate and work out either a new field instructor, new responsibilities, or a new practicum.)

Another student missed the first three meetings of her required weekly practicum seminar. She explained that this was necessary because she needed to work part time and had to schedule clients at the same time as the seminar. She couldn't understand why her faculty field liaison was unhappy with her lack of attendance. "After all," she said, "the agency staff are pleased with my performance." A third student managed to delight agency staff with his good humor and ability to work with children, but somehow he never found time to write his logs or document the number of hours he spent in the agency. His paperwork for his faculty field liaison was late by several weeks on each occasion that it was due.

Faced with situations such as these, it is easy to see how some students will distinguish themselves as being conscientious ("A") students and others will fall short of that mark. Neither agencies nor faculty field liaisons expect you to have supernatural abilities in order to succeed. Usually, success comes about through attention to details, such as completing assignments in a timely fashion, conforming to the expectations of the syllabus, showing up when expected in the agency, and displaying common courtesy.

Some practicum instructors use an evaluation form devised by Wilson (1981). She lists 20 professional/personal characteristics on which a student can be evaluated using behavioral expectations. Consider, for example, the characteristic she calls "Professional Responsibility." Students can be measured on this behavior along a continuum. A student with "A" behavior is "consistently responsible about all aspects of work and makes excellent use of time." An "F" student "appears bored with his work and puts self-interests first. Has a pattern of tardiness and/or absenteeism." Among the other 19 characteristics that Wilson suggests for the evaluation of students are:

Poise and Self-Control
Assertiveness
Personal Appearance as Related to Agency Standards
Effectiveness in Planning and Arranging Work Responsibilities
Ability to Assume Responsibility for Own Learning

Ability to Work Within the Purpose, Structure, and Constraints of the Agency and to Make Suggestions for Change in a Responsible Manner

Ability to Identify and Use Community Resources

Interviewing Skills, Including the Ability to Recognize and Interpret the Meaning of Nonverbal Communication

Written Communication Skills, Including the Ability to Record with Clarity and Promptness

Ability to Assess Situations Both Within and Outside the Client System and Determine Priorities

Ability to Develop and Maintain Professional Relationships with Consumers from Various Cultural, Ethnic, and Racial Backgrounds

Relationship with Co-workers (Other Students in the Agency as Well as Agency Staff)

Relationship with Staff of Other Agencies

Demonstration of the Acceptance and Use of Basic Social Work Values, Ethics, and Principles

Effectiveness in Providing Services to Individuals and Families

Effectiveness in Providing Services to Small Groups

Effectiveness in Providing Services at the Community Level

Use of Supervision

Development of a Professional Self-Awareness, Including the Need for Continued Professional Growth

Your faculty field liaison may use this or another scheme to evaluate your performance in the agency. Urbanowski and Dwyer (1988), for instance, have conceptualized criteria for field practice performance that vary slightly depending on whether the student is graduate or undergraduate, and if undergraduate, first or second semester. A sampling of these items is as follows:

First Semester Undergraduate
Functioning within the agency and community. The student begins to understand the structural components of the agency and has developed a good roster of social agency resources that would be helpful to clients.

Second Semester Undergraduate
Functioning within the agency and community. The student has comfort with the more commonly used policies and procedures and has the ability to interpret them clearly to clients and the community. The student organizes assignments so that maximum services are provided for all clients. Shows concern about obvious community problems.

First Semester Graduate
Functioning with the agency and community. The student knows the structure and function of the agency, and understands the administrative hierarchy and the process of decision making at the local agency level.

The student can make connections between the agency goals, policies, and procedures, and the services offered to clients. The student implements these services in accordance with the needs of the client and is aware of the inherent inequities in the overall social service system for special groups.

Second Semester Graduate

Functioning within the agency and community. The student assumes responsibility for continual learning about the agency and for creatively using the resources within it. The student has a solid knowledge about the operations of surrounding social systems and knows how to use these systems for the welfare of clients. The student is sensitive to the violation of clients' rights and explores action to remedy such situations.

How Do I Juggle All of My Roles Simultaneously?

During the course of a semester, many students experience anxiety from having to juggle too many roles and demands simultaneously. Studying and family responsibilities may conflict with work obligations, often causing a no-win situation. Whatever obligations they choose to meet, these pressured students may feel stress or guilt from omitting other, equally important obligations.

What can you do to reduce the problems caused by role conflicts? A good starting place is to consider your priorities. For example, if you are a parent, you will probably decide that the needs of your children have to come first. Taking care of sick children, preparing their meals, and finding time for them may be more important than getting all "A's." Likewise, you may have to learn how to let some household chores slide for a day or two so that you can study for an exam. "Something is going to have to give," one married undergraduate said, "I just can't do everything that I used to."

People who are well organized find it easier to juggle the additional roles of being a student and a practicum intern. You can assess your own level of organization. Disorganization may be suggested whenever you

> have frequent feelings of being behind and not caught up;
>
> procrastinate so long on an assignment that it becomes an emergency or panic situation;
>
> miss a deadline;
>
> misplace necessities such as car keys, glasses, or purse;
>
> have forgotten scheduled appointments, meetings, birthdays, or specific dates you wanted to remember;
>
> take more than 10 minutes to unearth a particular letter, bill, or report from your files (or from the piles of paper on your desk); or,
>
> are surprised at the end of most days by how little you have been able to accomplish.

If you identify with two or more of these items, then Winston (1978) suggests that you need help in developing organizational skills. She further recommends that you use three essential items for better organization: a day-by-day calendar, a pocket-sized notebook, and a daily to-do list. Use the calendar to record all appointments, deadlines, and crucial events. In your notebook, jot down errands and tasks you need to do as they occur to you. Think about your long- and short-term goals. Place on your to-do list and on your calendar the things that must be done in order for you to accomplish your goals. The to-do list should be compiled every day and should contain no more than 10 specific items. Winston advises rank ordering the items so that the most important are completed first.

Here are a few other suggestions for getting the most out of the time available to you: Find a few minutes each day so that you can plan. When you think about tomorrow, prepare to do the most difficult tasks first and at a time when you will be free from interruptions and can concentrate most effectively. Recently a student attending a social work convention asked the director of a large agency how he was able to supervise more than 80 employees. He replied that he came into the office at 6:30 every morning because he was able to get more paperwork and planning done between then and 8:30 than throughout the rest of the entire day. He purposefully looked for a quiet time in the agency and then put it to his full use.

Limit the number of outside activities that drain away your time while you are a student intern. Carefully consider requests being made of you. If you almost always say yes to additional projects or responsibilities outside of the practicum, try imposing a temporary moratorium. If it is difficult to refuse new requests, give yourself some time to think about them. If after you have done so you decide that it is not in your best interest to help, call and explain this. Keep your response simple and to the point. Inform others that you would like to help but simply do not have the time.

Try to avoid insignificant activities that clutter your life and distract you—for example, watching soap operas or game shows on television every evening before preparing for classes the next day.

Break large tasks into smaller segments. This will make the job seem much more manageable and will help you to avoid procrastination. For instance, if you have a 20-page term paper to write, plan to go to the library on Sunday. Create the outline for your paper on Monday. On Tuesday, write the introduction to the paper, and continue in this way to divide up the major task.

Despite good organizational skills, planning, and wise use of available time, most students occasionally experience high stress. It is important to know when you are under too much stress because it can affect your mental and physical health. Individuals react uniquely to stress, and you need to know how stress effects you. However, here are some common symptoms:

- inability to sleep;
- irritability;
- feeling pressured or ''smothering'';
- headaches and stomach aches;

- weight loss or gain;
- being tearful or more emotional; and
- being unable to concentrate or focus on a task.

Stress is not all bad. It can motivate you to get things done. However, too much stress can immobilize. When you sense you are approaching the limits of your ability to handle the stresses in your life, think about how you relax. What helps you to deal with stress? Here are some common ways to reduce daily stress:

- some type of physical activity (even walking);
- reading for pleasure;
- working in a garden or outdoors;
- mediation and prayer;
- playing with pets;
- having a conversation with a close friend;
- playing a musical instrument or listening to music;
- taking a short nap; and
- relaxation exercises.

If you are feeling highly stressed, bring the subject up in your integrative learning seminar and see if other students are feeling the same way. You may be surprised to learn that others are feeling just as stressed as you are. This group can serve in some ways as a support group for you. Also, it may assist you by suggesting resources or providing information that could help with a problematic client or situation. If there is a required seminar connected with your program, use it to your advantage. If, however, you have followed just about all of the suggestions provided here and you still have such a high level of stress that it is presenting problems for you, then it is time to seek a competent professional for assistance. Your field instructor or faculty field liaison can suggest professionals in the community for you to contact.

One final thought about juggling many roles: This situation can be viewed negatively or positively. On one hand, it could be seen as an "impossible" situation destined to create difficulties. On the other hand, it could be seen as an opportunity to develop better organizational skills while engaged in learning how to be a social worker. Having many commitments can actually work to your advantage by structuring your time. One graduate student explained,

When I have time available for studying, I don't waste a minute! I never put things off any more because I can't predict when one of my children might get sick or when my boss might ask me to work extra hours. Being a mother and an employee has actually helped me to prioritize my activities and to get the most out of the hours in my day.

The Student Intern's "Bill of Rights"

Sometimes when you are new to a situation it is hard to know whether your experiences are unique or similar to the experiences of others. Being a student intern differs from being a student in the classroom, and the newness of the internship experience and the responsibilities given to you may be almost overwhelming at times. If you are feeling this way, you may not be getting enough supervision from your field instructor. To give you some basis for grounding your experiences with what you are entitled, Munson (1987) has drafted a small set of rights to which practicum students are entitled:

1. The right to a field instructor who supervises them consistently at regularly designated times.
2. The right to a sufficient number and variety of cases to ensure learning.
3. The right to growth-oriented, as well as technical and theoretical, learning that is stable in its expectations.
4. The right to clear criteria for performance evaluation.
5. The right to a field instructor who is adequately trained and skilled in supervision. (pp. 105–106)

If you feel that your "rights" are being overlooked or violated, then discuss this matter with your faculty field liaison. On many occasions, faculty intervention can help to clarify responsibilities and smooth things out. And when necessary, it is the faculty field liaison's role to advocate for a student and to ensure that the student is not being mistreated, being given poor supervision, or ignored. Do not be afraid to consult with your faculty field liaison when your intuition or best judgment tells you that things are not right with your supervision or treatment in the agency. In the event that your faculty field liaison is the problem, discuss your difficulties with your academic adviser or the chairperson or academic head of your social work program.

IDEAS FOR ENRICHING YOUR PRACTICUM EXPERIENCE

1. As you find that you have blocks of unscheduled time in your agency, ask if you can visit other departments within the agency to learn what they do and about their clientele. Are there different eligibility considerations? Are there different fee schedules? Do the social workers in other departments have larger or smaller caseloads than those in the program where you have been assigned? How do their jobs vary?

2. If the agency where you have been assigned has volunteers, try to talk with several over lunch or during a break to learn about their contributions to the agency. Would services to clients be significantly affected if volunteers were not used? Considering the number of volunteers and the hours they contribute, what do you think is the value of their services? Are there other areas where volunteers could be used?

3. If there is a staff handbook or manual, read it as part of your orientation. Are there areas where the handbook is incomplete or needs to be expanded? Is there language to clarify the role of students? Are students treated more as nonpaid staff or as nonpaid volunteers?

4. Compare the evaluation form with which you will be evaluated with other examples that you can find (e.g., the one in Wilson's [1981] book, the personnel evaluation form used in the agency). Which form is the more comprehensive? From your reading of the evaluation form that your field instructor and faculty field liaison will use, is it clear over what areas you will be evaluated?

5. Is supervision a new experience for you? If so, what does it feel like? Has your field instructor identified any special skills or strengths that you didn't know you possessed? Keep a log of your feelings and the learning that occurs from sessions with your supervisor.

CASE VIGNETTES TO STIMULATE YOUR THINKING

Vignette A

Jim shows up for the 1st day of his practicum and finds that the agency is closed to clients. The whole agency is in a retreat because of a recent reorganization. He finds his faculty field instructor, who invites him to accompany her to a series of staff meetings. At times the discussion becomes heated. Junior staff members disagree with their supervisors. Jim does not think that this is proper and by noon is beginning to wonder if he has made a mistake in selecting this agency. By 3:00, however, things seem to have smoothed out and a genuine sense of camaraderie is evident. In fact, staff members have decided to come into the agency on Saturday, on their own time, to have a clean-up, fix-up day. Because their maintenance and improvement budget has been severely cut over the past 3 years, they intend to paint several offices on their own and to wash windows both inside and out.

QUESTIONS

Should Jim also volunteer to work on Saturday?
What would be the advantages of getting to know the staff members on an informal basis?
What if Jim already had plans to go out of town?
Should he feel that it is beneath his dignity to wash windows or paint?

Vignette B

Eileen decides to return to college after her children had gone on to college. At 45, she is the oldest student in her integrating seminar. Because of her maturity and good judgment, Eileen is placed in a very active social work department in a large metropolitan hospital. Very soon after her orientation, she is treated as a regular staff member—possibly because of an unfilled vacancy and the pregnancy leave of another social worker. Eileen is kept so busy on her practicum that she is often too busy to reflect or discuss with her agency supervisor what she has learned at the end of the day. On average, Eileen is working 1 or 2 hours extra each day she is in her practicum.

Usually, although not always, Eileen and her agency supervisor are able to find an hour once a week to talk. Eileen is beginning to resent having so much responsibility and so little time to study, read, and reflect as some of her classmates are finding time to do. Her supervisor has hinted that she knows Eileen is being given too much to do, but they are going to be short-handed for at least another 4 weeks. And, there is the possibility of a permanent job opening up for Eileen even while she is going to school. Eileen is torn between wanting to be considered for the vacant position and wanting to be treated as a student and not given quite so much responsibility.

QUESTIONS

Should Eileen have a "showdown" with her supervisor and complain about being overworked?

Is this best left to the faculty field liaison to work out?

Could Eileen be responsible and still cut back on her hours?

How would you cope in such a situation?

How do you cope with stress?

REFERENCES

Brill, N. (1990). *Working with people: The helping process.* White Plains, NY: Longman.

Egan, G. (1990). *The skilled helper: A systematic approach to effective helping.* Pacific Grove, CA: Brooks/Cole.

Munson, C. E. (1987). Field instruction in social work education. *Journal of Teaching in Social Work, 1*(1), 91–109.

Urbanowski, M. L., & Dwyer, M. M. (1988). *Learning through field instruction: A guide for teachers and students.* Milwaukee: Family Service America.

Wilson, S. (1981). *Field instruction: Techniques for supervisors.* New York: Free Press.

Winston, S. (1978). *Getting organized.* New York: Warner Books.

ADDITIONAL READINGS

Abbott, A. (1986). The field placement contract. *Journal of Social Work Education, 22*(1), 57–66.

Hamilton, N., & Else, J. F. (1983). *Designing field instruction: Philosophy, structure, and process.* Springfield, IL: Charles C. Thomas.

Johnson, H. W. (1988). Volunteer work in the introductory course: A special curriculum component. *Journal of Social Work Education, 24*(2), 145–150.

Maluccio, A., & Marlow, W. D. (1974). The case for the contract. *Social Work, 19*(1), 28–36.

Pfeiffer, J. W., & Jones, J. E. (1972). Criteria of effective goal-setting: The SPIRO model. In *The 1972 annual handbook for group facilitators.* La Jolla, CA: University Associates.

Randolf, J. L. (1982). The rights and responsibilities of clientele in field instruction. In B. W. Sheafor & L. E. Jenkins (Eds.), *Quality field instruction in social work.* White Plains, NY: Longman.

Reamer, F. G. (1989). Liability issues in social work supervision. *Social Work, 34*(5), 445–448.

CHAPTER 5

The Recipients of Service: Clients

Overview

Many social work students have never been required to ask for professional assistance or exposed to persons remarkedly poor, or different from their own families of origin. Like meeting a person from a foreign culture, questions arise about how best to communicate and work with these persons. This chapter seeks to provide help for students in understanding and working with unfamiliar clients.

What Is It Like to Be a Client?

Have you ever had a flat tire on a country road and then discovered that your spare was gone or that you had no jack? What would it be like to be in a strange city and accidentally lock your car keys and purse inside your car? Would you be comfortable stopping a complete stranger and asking for assistance? People who are accustomed to having resources (e.g., bank accounts, family members and friends willing to help, and a college education) sometimes find it difficult to imagine not having any of these. One seminary, in an effort to help new students to become more empathic with the problems of the homeless, took students to a nearby city and gave them just enough money to make one phone call (in the case of a true emergency). Students were to experience being homeless for 48 hours. Imagine how you would feel in such a situation. If it were an unfamiliar city and you were without a car or money, what emotions would you have? Would you be confused—not knowing where to go? Would you feel over-whelmed? Bewildered? Lost? Fearful?

We can assume that most clients are experiencing some significant problems and stress when they come into a social service agency. They want help with their problems and relief from the stress that they are experiencing. Many clients have never had to ask for assistance from anyone before, and they may not know exactly what kinds of help are available or whether or not they qualify.

Other clients have made use of agency services before and may know the rules and procedures better than you do. They may be impatient, demanding, or even rude. Their frustration may come from having to deal with impersonal bureaucrats, completing long application forms, or living on the barest minimum of economic assistance in a decaying and dangerous neighborhood. There may be court-ordered or involuntary clients. Many sources of stress or frustration may be compounded because most people find it difficult to ask for assistance from others.

We all react differently to stress, and clients are much like us, but often without our resources. Clients may view themselves as total failures because they had to ask for assistance with their problems. Some may feel silly or ridiculous. Others may feel totally confused—as when a tragic and unexpected situation has occurred. Take, for example, the woman who has just learned that her child has been sexually abused by the woman's husband. Imagine the range of emotions that the mother must feel—anger at the perpetrator, grief over the violation of the child (and possibly over the loss of an adult relationship), and guilt from not having been able to prevent the abuse. To these feelings we can add confusion over the best course of action (e.g., prosecution, divorce), and fear that the child has been permanently damaged or scarred.

When enough stress is heaped on some clients, they may break down and psychologically surrender. Many clients express a sense of being overwhelmed. They may become depressed, isolate themselves, and require help with problem-solving strategies. Certain clients will try to ignore or deny their problems and muddle through. Occasionally there are self-referred or voluntary clients who, after hesitating months or years, enter therapy with a great sense of urgency. For them, nothing can be done fast enough; they may pressure you to see them two or more times a week. In contrast, clients who are involuntary (because they have been mandated to seek help by a judge or officer of the court) may be hostile and uncooperative.

As a social work student in a practicum, it is important for you to accept each client as a unique human being who has immeasurable worth and dignity. You must understand the client's unique set of problems as the client experiences them. This entails being nonjudgmental and accepting of individual differences. Even if the client's problems are of his or her own making, you must realize that the client has needs which are not being met, and implement a plan to make the client more healthy or whole.

Occasionally, clients' problems will be so complex and convoluted that you will feel overwhelmed and inadequate. Even "simple" cases given to a student may later be found to be much more complicated than the presenting problem indicated. At any time that you feel inundated and unsure how to proceed, you should discuss this client with your agency supervisor. (Note that although for the majority of students a client may be one person, a client may also be a family, a group, an organization, or even a community.)

If you are interested in learning a little more about the helping process as seen through the client's eyes, you may want to read "He's Schizophrenic and the System Is Against Us: Reflections of a Troubled Parent and Professional," by Mona Wasow, or "Beyond 'Survival by Machine': Reflections of a Spouse" by Elizabeth Doolan with Toba Schwaber Kerson (both are contained in Kerson & Associates, 1989).

What Do Clients Expect from Me?

One of the joys (and sometimes one of the frustrations) of social work is that the profession exposes practitioners to many different types of people. Social work clients may be well educated and sophisticated, or have little education and be ill informed about what happens during the helping process. For instance, one client was overheard telling a friend that nothing happened during the 50-minute counseling session; she added, "All we did was talk."

Some clients are so limited in their ability to articulate family or individual dysfunctioning that they express their problems in terms of having "bad nerves." In their minds, complex problems can be solved with a prescription. As a result, they may request or even expect the social worker to provide physical relief of these symptoms by helping them to obtain a prescription for medication. Even if they don't anticipate pills, clients may anticipate rapid relief from the difficulties that brought them to the agency.

Clients completely unfamiliar with the process of counseling may be confused or may misunderstand the purpose of the social worker's questions. It may be necessary to inform them that social workers help clients by talking with them to discover more about their problems and strengths. However, the social worker cannot merely tell clients that intervention will consist mostly of talking, but may need to elaborate or provide concrete examples. Consumers of social work interventions may expect the social worker to do most of the talking and to *tell* them what to do or how to change their lives. They may not understand that social workers do not give this kind of advice.

Clients with a little more sophistication may expect that social workers will conduct the intervention by talking, but may have unrealistic expectations—hoping that all of the problems in their household will be resolved within 3 or 4 weeks. Because a social worker helped a friend, neighbor, or relative with a specific problem in a brief period of time, some clients may envision a "cure" in the same amount of time—not realizing the complexity of their cases or the difficulty in making comparisons with others.

Using your knowledge of human nature, you can anticipate all of the following:

1. Clients want to be treated as individuals and helped with their problems. Although not all clients expect immediate improvement in their life situations, most do not have the patience to wait months for the first signs of progress. Communicate some sense of hope that things will improve, but avoid making any promises that all of their problems will be resolved. Similarly, it is unwise to give specific dates by which clients can expect improvement.

2. Clients do not want to be inconvenienced. Usually, they want the initial interview to be scheduled without delay. They want the social worker to meet with them at convenient times, and they resent being kept waiting. Furthermore, they want the intervention to be as inexpensive as possible. These concerns need to be recognized.

3. Clients may be quite unaccustomed to talking about personal problems. They may have never told any other person about their feelings, hopes or dreams, sexual difficulties, or even mental illness within their families. During the helping process, you will be encouraging the client to learn not only that such topics can be discussed without embarrassment or crudity, but also that expressing painful feelings in a therapeutic environment brings about progress.

4. Clients expect you to be the authority—to guide the conversations, to ask the questions, and to act as if you are in charge. If you are too indecisive, then clients will perceive a lack of competence. Clients expect you to have better information about how to solve their problems than they have. They may also expect you to have specialized knowledge that you do not have. Often it is appropriate to tell the client that you don't have certain information. On other occasions, you may feel more comfortable telling the client that you will attempt to find the necessary information and will have it available at your next session. Don't allow clients to force you into the role of advice-giver. Clients must make their own choices.

5. Clients expect to be able to tell their problems to a sympathetic professional who will be sincere in trying to help them while protecting their confidentiality. If you were a client, wouldn't you want warm, empathic listening from someone who was neither judgmental nor critical? Listen attentively to each client. Don't stereotype clients or make hurried judgments. Treat every client as you would want to be treated.

Should I Inform Clients That I Am a Student?

Depending on where you live and the agency where you are placed, this problem may be solved for you during your orientation. For instance, the Massachusetts chapter of the National Association of Social Workers (NASW) has recommended that social work students identify themselves as trainees, interns, or students either verbally or by using name tags. An exception is made in emergency situations. It is also recommended that student status be designated in the signing of any notes in the official record. The general practice in most agencies across the United States is for the students' supervisors to countersign any agency records or documents signed by students.

In other states, the mandate to identify yourself as a student may not be quite as strong. Why? Because of the close supervision that they provide, some agencies have the philosophy that clients get no worse service, and sometimes even better service, from student interns than they get from regular staff members. In these agencies, clients would not routinely be informed of a student's status.

In one agency that comes to mind, clients who cannot afford private counseling are told that they may receive help from a student immediately or wait 6 to 10 weeks for a "free slot" to open up. Many clients choose students. In other agencies, the decision to inform clients may be left up to the student or to the student's agency supervisor.

Several authors have discussed the issue of informing clients about student status. Feiner and Couch (1985), for example, have considered many of the arguments for not informing clients but conclude that eliminating any secrecy about student status serves the profession better. Hepworth and Larsen (1990) support the position taken by Germain and Gitterman (1980) that students have an ethical responsibility to disclose their role to clients. Arguments for informing clients include these: Disclosure allows the student to be fully authentic in the relationship, and it will prevent problems later on during termination. Furthermore, it might be hard to keep this information from clients (e.g., clients may call at a time when students are not in the agency, and the receptionist might reply that they are unavailable but will be back from school by noon).

Certainly, students should not feel obligated to make self-deprecating remarks because they are students. Every professional has to start out as a student. Hepworth and Larsen (1990) suggest that instead of saying "I will see you for eight sessions because that is all of the available time before school ends," one should say, "I will see you for eight sessions because that is sufficient time" (p. 599). The latter provides for a more positive working relationship.

Although generally we believe that the student should identify himself or herself as such, common sense often is a reliable guide. A brief telephone inquiry by a potential client, for instance, probably will not necessitate that the intern identify his or her student status.

How Do I Know If I Am Helping My Clients?

Two clients from the graduate school days of one of the authors provide interesting illustrations for knowing when a client has been helped.

> The first client, a young woman, was brought into the community mental health clinic because of an inability to leave her home without fainting and experiencing a great deal of anxiety. The student soon discovered that the onset of the client's problem coincided with an incident when she had been brutalized by her former husband. He had kidnapped her from a parking lot and taken her to a remote spot, where he had tied her up and beaten her.
>
> The social work intervention consisted of empowering this woman by brainstorming and role-playing the courses of action open to her in any situation in which she might again encounter this person. (She could carry a police whistle, carry a can of mace, drive with her car doors locked, etc.) After about 6 weeks, the client indicated that she was doing better and did not need to continue in therapy. A short time later, it was learned that she was successfully employed in a department store. She had no further problems. It was obvious that this client had been helped.
>
> Another client had multiple problems and was resistant or unable to establish priorities for solving them. She was obese and had low self-esteem. Her intelligence

was slightly below normal. She had an alcoholic and unemployed husband, and was herself unemployed and occasionally abused drugs. The student displayed the same enthusiasm with this client as he had with the other client. He attempted to find her strengths and build on them.

The client's happy moments seemed to be largely associated with a period of time when a local motel employed her as a motel maid. She enjoyed the camaraderie of working with the other women and having a paying job. She felt sure that the motel people would hire her back again. However, by the end of the semester, absolutely no progress had been made. She was no closer to going back and asking for her old job than she had been the day she walked into the agency. She still had all sorts of domestic and personal problems. At the end of the summer, the student felt like a complete failure as he transferred the case to another social worker. This client obviously had not been helped at all.

The point of these two stories is that frequently there are very visible indicators that clients have improved (e.g., they quit drinking, secure employment, avoid getting into trouble with the law). Other times, it is practically impossible to detect any real growth or movement on the client's part. How is a student to evaluate the planned intervention?

Although the second of these two clients was more difficult and would have been a challenge for even an experienced social worker, the student would have had a greater probability of helping this client if clear objectives had been developed in the contract phase. Clients are often vague and have complaints such as, "I want to feel better about myself," or "I want to stop being so nervous." Sometimes they don't know exactly what is wrong except that they are feeling unhappy or blue. It is very hard to know when you have helped a client if the treatment goal is as ambiguous as to "help the client to feel better about self."

The key to knowing when you have helped a client is to identify a specific problem or behavior with which you can monitor improvement. If a client says, "I don't like myself," you need to ask, "How can I help?" or, "What are you doing when you begin thinking that you don't like yourself?" Such probing will usually lead to a specific behavior or situation that is troubling the client. For instance, the client who initially indicated that he did not like himself may be terribly shy and reluctant to begin dating even though a prospective date might be dropping numerous hints that she is interested. If the client would like himself better by securing the courage to begin dating, then focus the intervention on this. The criterion for success can be the client's securing that first date. Or, if the client doesn't know anyone interested in dating him, the target behavior may be having the client approach four different persons within a 30-day period and asking for a date.

Another client who says that he doesn't like himself may actually be expressing a desire to lose weight. You need to clarify this. If in fact the client is seriously overweight and believes he will like himself better if he can lose 65 pounds (and this seems to be his major concern), then the target behavior becomes the loss of weight.

Behaviors that can be monitored and reduced include angry outbursts, physical punishment of children, tardiness or absences from work, or instances of saying yes when the client really wanted to say no. Because psychometric scales exist for measuring certain attitudes or attitudinal traits, scales can be administered at the beginning and toward the end of intervention to see if clients have made gains in self-esteem or assertiveness, or if they are less depressed or anxious. (A number of instruments for monitoring improvement in clients are contained in Corcoran & Fischer's *Measures for Clinical Practice,* 1987.)

The systematic monitoring of a client's progress is a research method known as single-subject or single-system design. It is beyond the scope of this book to explain these techniques in detail, but you are referred to Berlin, 1983; Behling and Merves, 1984; or Royse, 1991, for more detailed instruction. However, the process essentially involves deciding on the target behavior to monitor, obtaining a baseline (an understanding of the frequency or stability of the behavior prior to intervention), beginning the intervention, and then recording or graphing any changes in the behavior. An illustration is presented in Figure 5.1.

What Do I Do When a Client Won't Talk?

First of all, clients who have been ordered to receive services from an agency are not likely to be in a cooperative mood. They may have been threatened with going back to jail, with the loss of a job, or with the child protection agency taking custody of their children. Because of racism, poverty, and other societal factors, clients may resent your being a part of the system that has restricted or regulated their activities. Mandated clients may know about others who have committed the same offense and yet received a lighter sentence from the court. Okay, so they are angry. What can you do about it?

Give the contentious client an opportunity to tell you why he or she is so angry, but first go over the ground rules explaining about confidentiality and what your role is. Be willing to listen to the client's side of the story. (Ask "what" questions that allow a client to describe a course of events instead of "how" or "why" questions that ask for an explanation.) Ask the client what help he or she needs or what assistance you can supply, then explain the intervention or assessment procedures. If the client is sullen and will not talk with you, then give the client permission not to talk. Do not threaten or attempt to force a client to talk. If beverages are available, asking the client to have something to drink might help to reduce tension and the formality of the situation. You might even take a moment or two over coffee to make small talk.

If the client still will not talk, without being parental, explain that the client can sit there the whole 50 minutes without talking—not talking is a legitimate choice available to every client. However, you hope this will not be the client's decision. With a warm, accepting smile convey that you will be glad to talk during this scheduled time, which is after all the client's time. If the client chooses not to talk, then you can put the time to good use by completing paperwork at your desk. Finally, give clients the agenda for next week so that they can have ample time to think about what they want to discuss. Be patient. Some clients find it hard to trust and to make new relationships.

Problem: Mrs. Smith's neighbors have reported her to child protection authorities because she frequently screams at her children. She is assigned to a social work intern for intervention.

Target Behavior: Parental screaming in the Smith household.

Baseline: A neighbor reported that Mrs. Smith screamed loudly at her young children at least on 20 separate occasions last week. Mrs. Smith does not deny that count. The baseline will be established at this point.[1]

Intervention: The dotted line after the 1st week indicates the beginning of intervention (see graph). Mrs. Smith is asked by the student intern assigned to her to keep a daily record of the number of times she loses patience and screams at her children. She is assessed as being quite motivated to learn more about parenting. Mrs. Smith readily agrees to attend classes on child care and to keep a tally of her verbal outbursts.

Explanatory Note: As you can see from the graph, Mrs. Smith has made steady progress in learning how to deal with the stress of being a parent and not exploding verbally at her children. It is quite clear from this graph that the student who had been working with Mrs. Smith was very successful in helping her to reduce the frequency of the target behavior.

Instances of Screams and
Verbal Abuse of Children

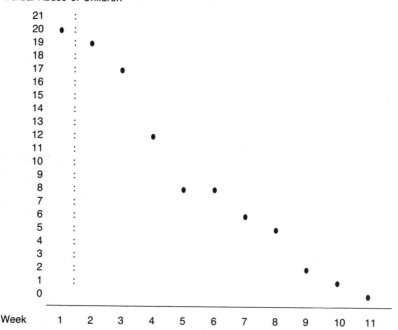

Week

[1] Sometimes it may take 3 or 4 weeks to develop a good understanding of a problem and its severity, but in this example we are using an abbreviated baseline.

FIGURE 5.1 Single-Subject Design for Intervention with Mrs. Smith

What Do I Do When the Client Who Won't Talk Is a Child?

When clients are children, the office setting may be much more anxiety producing. You may have to reassure the child that the two of you just need to talk for a little while. If the child is particularly fearful, then acknowledge that children sometimes are a little scared at first, but that they soon forget that when they find how easy it is to talk to you. If after this explanation the child still will not answer any questions, do not show any frustration or anger—instead say, "That's okay. Let's do something different." Any agency that regularly has children for clients should have some toys available. Show the toys to the child and say, "I wonder what you'd like to play with." Gabel, Oster, and Pfeffer (1988) suggest that at this point the child may through nonverbal invitation involve you in the play and then begin talking. Sometimes you can encourage this by parallel play, or by making occasional remarks. If this does not work, they advise making something interesting from modeling clay or from paper and crayons. Ask for comments about what you are doing. Realize that with this type of child, the relationship will be built gradually and possibly require several sessions before the child feels comfortable enough to talk. If after your best efforts the child still will not communicate, try bringing in one or more family members to be with the child. Anxiety may be lessened when the child observes how other family members can converse with you without adverse results.

What Do I Do with Angry and Hostile Clients?

It is not uncommon for social workers to find themselves confronted with angry and potentially dangerous clients. Often these are involuntary clients who resent being forced into involvement with a social service agency. Unfortunately, you may become the "displaced object of resentment" (Hepworth & Larsen, 1990). Although their anger may not be directed to you as a person, you certainly may feel its heat and want to react defensively. Dealing with such clients requires a cool head and presence of mind in addition to familiarity with techniques that diffuse explosive situations.

First of all, try your best to stay calm and composed. Remind yourself that the client's anger may be natural and understandable given the situation. The client may have strong feelings of injustice. The system may have been too impersonal, bureaucratic, or inflexible. Because you represent the system to the client, he or she may be taking advantage of finding a sympathetic ear to unload anger and frustrations that have been building over time.

As much as possible, try to be empathic and understanding. Allow these clients to talk and explain why they are so angry. Speak in a soft voice and move slowly. Sheafor, Horejsi, and Horejsi (1988) recommend that you avoid touching an angry client or moving into his or her personal space. Sit if you can; standing is a more aggressive position. (However, do not position yourself in a corner or behind furniture, where it would be difficult to get out if escape becomes necessary.) Encourage the client to sit.

By not reflecting back the client's anger, you should be able to influence the client's behavior positively. More than likely, the client will be watching how you react, so you need to be aware of how your actions can be interpreted. If the client is agitated, use the same techniques that you would use for a nervous client; for instance, ask if you can get the client a cup of coffee or something to drink. Trust your intuition. If you sense that you are in danger of being hurt, get out of that situation as quickly and cooly as possible. Say that you need a drink of water, or that you have to check on something—then leave the room and seek help.

Above all else, do not take risks that will jeopardize your personal safety. If your intuition tells you that a situation is dangerous, do not plow headstrong into it because you don't want to be embarrassed that you couldn't handle it. Always seek help when you sense that your safety or that of others is in danger. Discuss with your field instructor and other staff members your apprehensions in order to get feedback on how to handle difficult situations. Such conversations may allay your fears or give you suggestions for ensuring your safety.

Similarly, use good judgment when planning to make a home visit by yourself or when traveling into high crime areas. Consider taking another person along whenever you expect to be in hazardous areas, and arrange for a police officer to accompany you whenever entering potentially volatile or risky situations in the community. Routinely when traveling outside of the agency, keep someone informed of your destination, the length of time you expect to be there, and the time you expect to arrive back at the agency. If your appointment is at the end of the day or after dark, have an agreement with the person to whom you tell your destination that you will call when you have arrived safely back home.

How Do I Work with Clients Who Are Different from Me?

You can expect in a social service practicum to encounter many different kinds of clients. They may differ in terms of religious beliefs, skin color, age, sexual preference, lifestyle, native language or country of origin, socioeconomic class, and hundreds of ways that are not easily anticipated. You may discover physicians who are wife beaters, social workers who are alcoholics, and clergy who are adulterers. Many of your idealized images or stereotypes about people will undoubtedly be shattered as you learn that all humans have the same basic needs and foibles.

Maslow (1970) has helped us to understand that in addition to food, water, oxygen, and safety, we all have needs to belong and love, to achieve and be competent, and to fulfill our unique potential. We need others to value or appreciate us and to think that we are important. These things are essential, no matter what our skin color, gender, or native language. We can always relate to other human beings when we think about the things that we have in common. Although we may differ on what constitutes the "good life," most of us want to be safe and secure, to have enough food, to have our loved ones around us, to have access to medical care and entertainment, and to have outlets for work or creative expression.

Sometimes, however, it is possible to "universalize" too much. Not everyone will like the same foods or seasonings that you like, nor agree with your notion of the best presidential candidate or the best religion, nor express his or her sexuality in the same way as you. We all have common human needs, but as human beings we differentiate ourselves from others. Some of these differences are cultural (e.g., the foods we eat), some are acquired in the process of living and growing up, and others may be learned unconsciously. Clients' unique needs are the result of the interplay of individual and cultural factors.

In order to work effectively with clients, social workers must recognize, understand, and accommodate both their universal and unique needs. Ignorance of a client's culture has to be overcome consciously. Students can learn about the unique characteristics of others by reading, observing, listening, and being sensitive to the fact that not everyone will have the same preferences and values.

Until you understand them better, you may find that clients from different cultures or backgrounds are not as open with you as they may be with other staff. Because of language difficulty or other factors that make you feel uncomfortable around them, they may sense that you do not accept them. If a client from another culture is resistant, ask yourself if you are viewing the client in a stereotypical manner or judging him or her from your own cultural or socioeconomic values. If the answer is yes, then you will probably want to talk with more experienced staff members or your field instructor about approaches or techniques to try with this client. Do not rely blindly on standard counseling techniques with clients from other cultures without questioning whether these or other techniques are more appropriate. At a minimum, do some reading on how to work with this population. (Some useful resources include Brislin, Cushner, Cherrie, & Yong, 1986; Chau, 1990; Davis & Proctor, 1989; Devore & Schlesinger, 1987; Dhooper & Tran, 1987; Garland & Escobar, 1988; Gettman & Pena, 1986; Hardman, 1975; Jacobs & Bowles, 1988; Lum, 1986; and Morales, 1981.)

When working with people who have different values, it is probably inevitable that some clash will occur. Such incidents present opportunities for students to examine their own values. It is helpful to remember that professional values take precedence over personal values. Social workers do not have the right to impose their religious or moral values on others. Ethical practice entails making the welfare of the client the primary obligation and providing service that is nondiscriminatory. Every client is entitled to fairness, equal access to services, respect, impartiality, confidentiality, empathy, and a nonjudgmental attitude (see Siporin, 1975, for a discussion of ethical practice principles). When unable to treat, with an open and impartial attitude, a particular client or clients who have specific characteristics or problems, the students need to discuss their possible prejudices or biases with their field instructor or faculty field liaison. Students who allow biases and prejudices against other persons to interfere with the quality of care provided to clients will be in violation of professional ethics. Unless they are willing to do some intensive self-examination and make a mighty effort to accept diverse clients, these students should seriously consider another line of work.

What Are the Limits of Confidentiality?

Most social work students, by the time they are ready to start a practicum, have been well drilled or indoctrinated on the importance of respecting confidentiality. From the NASW Code of Ethics (reprinted as Appendix B), students have learned to hold in confidence all information obtained in the course of professional service and to share information revealed by clients with others only when there are compelling professional reasons. The NASW Code of Ethics further states that clients should have access to records concerning them; that care should be taken to protect the confidences of others contained in those records; and that the social worker should obtain the informed consent of clients before taping, recording, or permitting third-party observation of their activities.

By the start of the practicum, students have learned that the term *confidentiality* in a social service agency generally refers to relative confidentiality, not absolute confidentiality. The Federal Privacy Act of 1974 makes it clear that information regarding clients and staff may be shared with officers and employees of the agency who have a need for such records in the performance of their duties (Wilson, 1978). That information revealed by a client can be subpoenaed for use in court also helps students to understand the concept of relative confidentiality.

Unquestionably, there are times when information obtained from clients should be shared with others. The client's right to confidentiality does not extend to the abuse or harm of children. All 50 states now have statutes that require professionals to report any suspected child abuse or neglect. In some states, professionals are also required to report elder abuse. Similarly, if a client makes a serious threat of suicide, or homicide, this information should be shared with other professionals and family members even if it violates confidentiality (see Chapter 6).

Guidelines for violating the client's confidentiality are not well defined. For instance, if a client threatens a criminal act (e.g., a man says he is going to beat up his wife), many professionals would weigh the seriousness of the crime and abandon the principle of confidentiality only to prevent serious harm. Using this criterion, illegal activities such as the use of marijuana or engaging in prostitution do not justify breaking confidentiality. When confronted with a dilemma about breaching a client's confidentiality, it is always necessary to discuss your next course of action with your agency supervisor. Certainly, disclosure without a client's permission should take place only under the most extreme circumstances and only as a last resort (Reamer, 1991).

Relative confidentiality can also be seen in the way that researchers, evaluators, and quality assurance personnel read case records or parts of these records to determine which clients are benefiting from intervention, and the characteristics of clients enrolled in selecting programs. Generally, clients must give their permission in order to participate in a research or evaluation project. However, if the nature of the research or evaluation relies on closed cases or historical data, then client permission generally is not sought, provided that personal identifying information (e.g., the client's name, address, or phone number) is not to be obtained or used and that the research methodology does not involve contacting clients.

Occasionally, social work students may be asked to make a case presentation to one of their classes or seminars. In such situations, sharing details of a case is not a violation of the client's confidentiality if you do not give out any personal identifying information. Do not describe famous or notorious clients in such a way that they can be recognized. Instead, be somewhat general in your description and try to change a few personal details. You might say, for instance, that the client is a 40-year-old mother of four with a professional career, married to a college graduate, who has been referred from the courts for a first-time shoplifting offense. If you find it necessary to refer to the client by a name, make one up or refer to the client by some initial (e.g., ''Mrs. B'').

Descriptions that could fit any number of people in the community because they do not identify the client are not a violation of clients' confidentiality when used within a professional or educational context. However, the more times you repeat a description, the greater the likelihood that someone might be able to recognize your client. For this reason, professionalism requires that even brief, general descriptions of clients not be shared at parties and social occasions.

The same discretion is expected if you should identify a client from another student's presentation. Occasionally during classes or seminars, a client who receives services from more than one agency will be recognized by one or more students who know each other. Whenever this happens, you are bound by the same principle of confidentiality as is the student assigned the case and making the presentation.

Confidentiality is a complex subject that can be covered only superficially in this section. You may want to consult additional readings (Abramson, 1990; Alperin, 1989; Jacobs, 1991; Lindenthal, Jordan, Lentz & Thomas, 1988; Reamer, 1991; Schwartz, 1989; Watkins, 1989; Whittington, 1988).

IDEAS FOR ENRICHING YOUR PRACTICUM EXPERIENCE

1. Are there any 1 or 2 day workshops or seminars being offered close by that would improve your social work skills? If so, ask your field instructor for permission to attend appropriate workshops. If there is a fee for these workshops and you can't afford to attend, then contact the persons conducting the workshops to see if there are scholarships or if you can attend by working (e.g., helping with the registration table).

2. If there are no workshops or seminars being conducted close by, then visit the agency library and find out the major journals to which they subscribe. Browse these for interesting articles that may help with the clients you have been assigned. If your agency does not have its own library, then ask your field instructor for the journals that he or she reads or that are recommended for you to read. Leaf through these in your university's library.

3. Select one of your clients and draw up a single-subject design as discussed in this chapter. Are your intervention goals narrow enough that it is easy to specify a target behavior to be changed?

4. Ask if a program evaluation has been conducted recently for the program under which you are interning. Read the evaluation to see how successful the program is. What recommendations did the evaluators make? What recommendations would you make?

5. Determine if within your agency there is a staff person assigned to do community education. If possible, accompany this person to a public speaking engagement as a way of learning more about the agency. If no one in the agency tends to do any public speaking, then try to find out why not. In what way might the agency benefit from organizing a speaker's bureau?

CASE VIGNETTES TO STIMULATE YOUR THINKING

Vignette A

Walking to class one day, a fellow social work student informs you that he could never work with gay or lesbian clients. He says that he would get rid of them as quickly as possible if he were ever assigned this type of client. You are too stunned to reply. You sense that this student is terribly homophobic. You wonder whether this student has ever read the NASW Code of Ethics.

QUESTIONS

As a fellow student, what would you do?

What would you do if you were the student's field instructor?

Would the situation be any different if the student had said that he couldn't work with African Americans?

What if he had said that he couldn't work with alcoholics or child molesters?

Vignette B

The intake secretary motions for you to come over to her desk one afternoon. In a hushed voice she tells you to expect a client tomorrow who is going to be "angry, demanding, and obnoxious." Although you know that clients are not always going to be pleasant and enjoyable to work with, several times that afternoon your mind goes back to what the secretary said. In preparation, you pull Mrs. Havolec's case record and read it. She has been a client on at least four different occasions—always presenting with a different problem and always terminating on her own against professional advice. Usually she stops coming to the agency when it appears she may be on the verge of making some significant progress. She is a chronic client, and there are ample notes attesting to her being grouchy and quick tempered. Your reading of her record also uncovers that she seems to be the most ill-humored with the receptionist and that she becomes more agreeable and congenial when she interacts with persons of greater authority and status. You wonder whether you should bend the agency's policy and not inform Mrs. Havolec tomorrow that you are a student.

QUESTIONS

In the interest of getting along better with the client, would it be okay to wait a couple of sessions or so to inform Mr. Havolec that you are a student?

What would you do if Mrs. Havolec demanded (after spending 15 minutes with you) to be transferred to another worker?

Would you feel comfortable asking her to give you a fair chance—to wait at least another 45 minutes or so before deciding she had to have another worker?

REFERENCES

Abramson, M. (1990). Keeping secrets: Social workers and AIDS. *Social Work, 35*(2), 169–173.

Alperin, D. E. (1989). Confidentiality and the BSW field work placement process. *Journal of Social Work Education, 25*(2), 98–108.

Berlin, S. B. (1983). Single-case evaluation: Another version. *Social Work Research and Abstracts, 19*(1), 3–11.

Behling, J. H., & Merves, E. S. (1984). *The practice of clinical research: The single case method.* New York: University Press of America.

Brislin, R. W., Cushner, K., Cherrie, C., & Yong, M. (1986). *Intercultural interactions: A practical guide.* Beverly Hills, CA: Sage.

Chau, K. L. (1990). Social work practice: Towards a cross-cultural practice model. *Journal of Applied Social Sciences, 14*(2), 249–275.

Corcoran, K., & Fischer, J. (1987). *Measures for clinical practice: A sourcebook.* New York: Free Press.

Davis, L. & Proctor, E. (1989). *Race, gender, and class: Guidelines for practice with individuals, families, and groups.* Englewood Cliffs, NJ: Prentice-Hall.

Devore, W., & Schlesinger, E. G. (1987). *Ethnic-sensitive social work practice.* Columbus, OH: Merrill.

Dhooper, S. S., & Tran, T. V. (1987). Social work with Asian Americans. *Journal of Independent Social Work, 1*(4), 51–62.

Feiner, H. A., & Couch, E. H. (1985). I've got a secret: The student in the agency. *Social Casework, 66*(5), 268–274.

Gabel, S., Oster, G., & Pfeffer, C. R. (1988). *Difficult moments in child psychotherapy.* New York: Plenum Medical.

Garland, D. R., & Escobar, D. (1988). Education for cross-cultural social work practice. *Journal of Social Work Education, 24*(3), 229–241.

Germain, C., & Gitterman, A. (1980). *The life model of social work practice.* New York: Columbia University Press.

Gettman, D., & Pena, D. G. (1986). Women, mental health, and the workplace in a transnational setting. *Social Work, 31*(1), 5–11.

Hardman, D. G. (1975). Not with my daughter, you don't! *Social Work, 20*(4), 278–285.

Hepworth, D. H., & Larsen, J. A. (1990). *Direct social work practice.* Belmont, CA: Wadsworth.

Jacobs, C. (1991). Violations of the supervisory relationship: An ethical and educational blind spot. *Social Work, 36*(2), 130–135.

Jacobs, C., & Bowles, D. D. (1988). *Ethnicity and race: Critical concepts in social work.* Silver Spring, MD: National Association of Social Workers.

Kerson, T. S., & Associates (1989). *Social work in health settings: Practice in context.* New York: Haworth Press.

Lindenthal, J. J., Jordan, T. J., Lentz, J. D., & Thomas, C. S. Social workers' management of confidentiality. *Social Work, 33*(2), 157–159.

Lum, D. (1986). *Social work practice and people of color.* Pacific Grove, CA: Brooks/Cole.

Maslow, A. (1970). *Motivation and personality.* New York: Harper & Row. (Originally published 1954.)

Morales, A. (1981). Social work with third-world people. *Social Work, 26*(1), 45–51.

Reamer, F. G. (1991). AIDS, social work, and the "duty to protect." *Social Work, 36*(1), 56–60.

Royse, D. (1991). Single system designs. In *Research methods for social workers.* Chicago: Nelson-Hall.

Schwartz, G. (1989). Confidentiality revisited. *Social Work, 34*(3), 223–226.

Sheafor, B. W., Horejsi, C. R., & Horejsi, G. A. (1988). *Techniques and guidelines for social work practice.* Boston: Allyn & Bacon.

Siporin, M. (1975). *Introduction to social work practice.* New York: Macmillan.

Takaki, R. (1987). *From different shores: Perspectives on race and ethnicity in America.* New York: Oxford University Press.

Watkins, S. A. (1989). Confidentiality and privileged communications: Legal dilemma for family therapists. *Social Work 34*(2), 133–136.

Whittington, R. (1988). "Button your lips!" *Journal of Independent Social Work, 3*(2), 93–100.

Wilson, S. J. (1978). *Confidentiality in social work: Issues and principles.* New York: Free Press.

ADDITIONAL READING

Corey, M. S., & Corey, G. (1989). Dealing with difficult clients. In *Becoming a helper.* Pacific Grove, CA: Brooks/Cole.

CHAPTER **6**

The Student Intern: Needed Skills

Overview

This chapter is designed to help students feel less nervous about beginning to work with their clients by providing a brief refresher on topics usually covered in students' practice courses.

Do Most Student Interns Feel Nervous and Inadequate?

Yes, probably a majority of students beginning a new social work practicum experience some anxiety. Anxiety before starting a practicum does not indicate that students are not suited for social work, only that they want to do well and are aware that they have much still to learn. Changes in routines and new experiences involve an element of risk that is always a little scary. Consciously or unconsciously student interns may think, "What if I don't do well in this placement?" "What if my agency supervisor is too critical or expects too much?" "What if I can't help my clients?" or "Should I have taken additional classes before registering for the practicum?" In a recent study we conducted, almost half of the students going into a practicum expressed concern about their competence to perform clinical interventions and the belief that additional skills were needed. Understandably, undergraduate students going into their first practicum were more anxious than students who had been in a prior practicum.

Logistical concerns can also be a source of anxiety. Questions may surface such as, What if traffic is terrible and I am late the first day?" "What if I can't find a parking spot?" or "Where will I go for lunch?" These concerns can usually be managed by thinking ahead. To plan for the length of time it takes to travel, students can, for instance, drive to the agency a time or two in rush hour traffic.

They can look for a parking lot near the agency, or call the agency supervisor beforehand and ask where to park. And, students can always pack a lunch for the first day until they discover where others in the office eat.

The important thing to realize is that it is okay to feel anxious—it is a common experience—and that making specific plans often helps to reduce some of the anxiety. In a book we recommend for students, Corey and Corey (1989) share some of their initial experiences in starting out:

> In one of my earlier internships I was placed in a college counseling center. I remember how petrified I was when one day a student came in and asked for an appointment, and my supervisor asked me to attend to this client. . . . Some of the thoughts that I remember running through my head as I was walking to my office with this client were, "I'm not ready for this. What am I going to do? What if he doesn't talk? What if I don't know how to help him? I wish I could get out of this!" (p. 11)

Such anxieties and concerns are normal and all right for students to experience, because as social workers they will often have to support clients when they make changes in their lives. It is good for students to recall their own feelings when encountering change and new situations.

What Skills Might I Be Expected to Develop?

The diversity of human problems and their manifestation at different levels—individual, group, neighborhood, community, institutional, and societal—create the breadth of social work as a profession. Accordingly, different methods, approaches, and strategies have been conceived so that intervention can be applied in various situations and contexts.

The basic problem-solving method taught in practice courses is applicable across all situations and provides the basis for deciding how to intervene. Similarly, there are skills common to all levels of human organization. These include listening, observing, relationship building, interviewing, assessing, contracting, mediating, advocating, planning, and evaluating. Anticipating that most students are going to be doing practicums in agencies where the major focus is on the problems of individual clients, we have devoted more space to the discussion of skills appropriate at the micro level of intervention. Nevertheless, we also want students to see the larger picture where macro interventions are appropriate—the client's problems in relationship to the agency, the community, and society.

Community organization refers to various methods of intervention whereby a worker helps a collection of individuals to engage in planned action for dealing with a common social problem. The major tasks include identifying problems, analyzing factors that cause those problems, formulating plans, developing strategies, mobilizing resources, and implementing, monitoring, and evaluating the plans. Rothman (1968) has proposed three models of community organization practice: locality development, social planning, and social action—each requires some common and some specific strategies, tactics, and roles. Often known as macro practice, community organization activities can include the administration of social agencies, interagency coordination, fundraising, political action, and public education campaigning. Even in an agency that serves individuals and families, students will be able to practice some community organization skills. Most social service agencies are involved in interagency case conferences, social service planning activities, and public education projects.

Advocacy is championing the rights of others through direct intervention or by empowering clients to represent themselves. The NASW Code of Ethics states that advocacy is a basic social work obligation to society—that ethical behavior requires acting to prevent or eliminate discrimination, to ensure equal access to services and opportunities, and to bring about changes in policy or legislation that improve social conditions and promote social justice. However, social service agencies and institutions sometimes create limitations on the practice of advocacy within the organization because of political implications related to funding bodies and public support. During the 1980s governmental efforts to ensure the quality of services provided to specific client groups resulted in greater case management and case advocacy.

Case management attempts to coordinate health and social services on behalf of a client or group of clients generally requiring long-term care. Case management involves screening, assessing, consulting, care plan developing, arranging for services, as well as coordinating and monitoring the client and the delivery of services. These activities are oriented toward eliminating the fragmentation that can occur when clients need multiple services.

Hopefully, this brief introduction will help you to think of the diversity of skills that social workers practice. You are encouraged to ask your field instructor to structure opportunities for you to develop macro-level skills as well as micro-level ones.

We expect that most students entering a practicum for the first time will be practicing micro-levels skills. Although some students may go into macro-level placements without ever developing the skills required for working with individual clients, we think that this would be rare. Most students start on the ground floor by learning how to work with clients one-on-one. The balance of this chapter will focus on the skills and problems that may arise in traditional clinical treatment settings.

How Do I Start Interviewing with a Client?

According to Kadushin (1972), social workers spend more time interviewing than in any other activity. It is the most important, most frequently employed, social work skill. In view of its importance, it is natural for student interns to feel somewhat uneasy whenever they begin to think about the responsibility of interviewing that first client. So relax a bit if you feel uneasy—the majority of students (and probably clients, too) face the first interview with some apprehension.

It may help to realize that the physical environment gives you some measure of control during the interview. Freedom from distraction, privacy, and open space between participants in a room with comfortable furniture and adequate ventilation and light will make it easier for the client and for you. Check the interviewing room ahead of time (if the room is different from your office) to ensure that the temperature setting is comfortable and that there will be enough chairs (e.g., if a family is expected). Sit in the room and get accustomed to it. Think of the questions you will need to ask. If you do not feel at ease there (e.g., because it is too hot or cold, or has insufficient privacy), then try to arrange for another office before the client arrives.

In a quiet office it is easier to feel relaxed, and to listen thoughtfully and give the client your full attention. Consider the arrangement of the furniture and whether it is better to sit behind the desk or away from it. Sitting behind a desk emphasizes the authority of the social worker and lends more formality to the meeting. Sitting away from the desk may help to create rapport a little more quickly.

An interview can be conceptualized as a three-stage process: (1) the opening or beginning stage, (2) the middle or working- together stage, and (3) the termination stage. Each has a different focus and different tasks to be accomplished. Let's look at each of these stages in more depth.

The beginning stage starts when the interviewer greets the client, does whatever will make the client comfortable, and defines the purpose of the interview. Think of interviewing as a purposeful conversation. There is a specific purpose and reason why you will be talking with the client. However, the purpose may not always be known to the client (e.g., a court-referred client). After introducing yourself, therefore, it is often a good idea to ensure that the client is clear on the purpose of the interview. Always give the client an opportunity to discuss the purpose and any special needs. In the initial interview, the intent is generally to learn about the client, the problem, and the efforts that have been made to solve the problem; to identify untapped resources that may exist; and to find out what the client's expectations are of the worker and the agency.

It is safe to assume that the client has questions about the helping process (e.g., how the helping will occur, how long it will take, what it will cost). Such questions may not be asked directly but might be anticipated. Imagine yourself as a client in a strange agency seeking help for a comparable problem. What questions come to mind? Answering these questions, and pointing out that the agency exists to help clients with this type of problem, will help to break the ice. Asking for help from strangers is not always easy, and in this phase it is important to help clients feel that they are in the right place and have made the correct decision.

As both of you begin to feel more comfortable, encourage the client to verbalize his or her feelings about the problem situation. An age-old social work maxim, "Begin where the client is," suggests that you attempt to understand the problem from the client's perspective. Avoid going into the interview with a preconceived idea about what the client is like or is apt to say. Do not form opinions too early or become guilty of stereotyping the client and hearing only what you have decided he or she will be saying.

Even while introducing yourself and describing the agency's policies, programs, and resources, convey an interest and a willingness to understand the client's point of view. Each of your communications should reflect an interest in the client. For instance, gently probe, inquire, guide, and suggest. Do not cross-examine, make accusations or demands, or dominate. Both verbal and nonverbal messages should express an interest in the client.

The character of the case and the personal characteristics of the client will influence the interviewing process. With some types of problems, you will need to proceed more slowly than with others. The middle stage of the interview process is purpose-specific. You will be monitoring your communications for their effectiveness in keeping the interview on course, refocusing the client if the interview begins to drift away from its purpose, and possibly renegotiating a contract if that is indicated. When the purpose of the interview has been fulfilled, or just before the agreed time for ending the interview has been reached, the interview has reached the third stage.

During the termination stage, summarize what has happened during the interview. Agree on the next step (including the work to be done before the next interview and the purpose, time, and place of the next interview). Kadushin (1972) advises,

> In moving toward the end there should be a dampening of feeling, a reduction in intensity of affect. Content that is apt to carry with it a great deal of feeling should not be introduced toward the end of the interview. The interviewees should be emotionally at ease when the interview is terminated. (p. 208)

Usually it is appropriate to engage in a few minutes of social conversation as a transition out of the interview.

Sheafor, Horejsi, and Horejsi (1988) suggest some helpful guidelines for interviewing:

1. Be prepared to respond in an understanding way to the client's fears, ambivalence, confusion, or anger during the first meeting.
2. Be aware of your own body language. The way you are dressed, your posture, facial expressions, and hand gestures all send messages to the client. Try to send a message of respect and caring.
3. If you have only limited time to spend with a client, explain this at the beginning of the session so the things of highest priority will receive attention.
4. Give serious attention to the presenting problem, as described by the client, but realize that many clients will test your competency and trustworthiness before revealing the whole story or the "real" problem. Begin with whatever the client considers important and wants to talk about.
5. Adapt your language and vocabulary to the client's capacity to understand.
6. If you do not understand what the client is saying, ask for further clarification or an example.
7. When you do not know the answer to a question asked by the client, explain so in a nonapologetic manner and offer to find the answer.
8. Explain the rules of confidentiality that apply to your meeting, and be certain to inform the client if what he or she says cannot be held in complete confidence.
9. If the client is bothered by your note-taking, explain why [notes] are needed, what will happen with [them], and offer to show the notes you have taken. If the client still objects, cease note-taking. If you are completing a form

or following an outline, give the client a copy of the form to follow along with you.

10. Before the interview ends, be sure that the client has your name and the agency phone number, and that you have the client's full name, address, and phone number. (pp. 197–198)

To these we add a few of our own guidelines that will make it easier for clients to trust and feel that you are professional:

1. Never lie to a client or pretend that you have experience that you do not.
2. Do not make promises that you may not be able to keep or promises on behalf of others.
3. Do not argue with clients.
4. Do not attempt to force a client to tell you something that he or she does not want to tell. (If either you or the client are making frequent use of the word but, then you are probably forcing some idea or line of questioning on the client. This will be experienced as more of an interrogation than an interview.)
5. Do not display (verbally or nonverbally) shock, surprise, or disbelief in response to what a client may tell you.
6. Do not talk down to a client or try to impress the client with your knowledge of clinical terms or jargon.
7. Although you may run out of time, do not rush the client. Realize that hesitation may be the result of anxieties or fears. Furthermore, do not finish sentences or supply words for clients in an effort to speed them up. If necessary, make a second appointment to complete the interview.

If, after reading this section, you still feel the need to do some extra preparation, then consult some of the texts on interviewing at the end of the chapter, or obtain a workbook such as Cournoyer's (1991) *The Social Work Skills Workbook.*

How Do I Begin to Help the Clients Who Are Assigned to Me?

Having acknowledged that you may feel a little insecure in your ability to help clients, let's quickly review what you should already know about the helping process:

1. The social worker makes use of self in helping clients. *Self* includes the knowledge acquired from the traditional academic environment, the common sense developed as a result of life experiences, and the social worker's personality. Social workers help clients to solve their problems through techniques such as listening, leading, reflecting, summarizing, confronting, interpreting, and informing. They support, explore alternatives, model behavior, teach, and sometimes refer (see Brammer, 1985).

To help others, social workers need to be self-aware. They must know their own values, biases, strengths, and limitations. In reviewing the training of family therapists, Bagarozzi and Anderson (1989) discuss the sense of self as a primary vehicle for therapeutic change,

> often evidenced in less of a tendency to "do things to and for clients" or to "give clients an intervention" and more of an emphasis on "being with clients" or "responding" to clients with greater genuineness, honesty, openness and courage. (p. 284)

The necessary skills and knowledge to help clients are not easily specified—and probably reflects a constellation of abilities, knowledge, and experiences. Some social work students will be more aware of themselves than others; some will be more knowledgeable or more experienced. Many students can, however, make up for most real or presumed deficiencies in their expertise by being an active and interested participant in the helping process. Egan (1990) writes,

> The best helpers are active in the helping sessions. They keep looking for ways to enter the worlds of their clients, to get them to become more active in the sessions, to get them to own more of it, to help them see the need for action—action in their heads and action outside their heads—in their everyday lives. (p. 105)

2. The first step in helping any client is the establishment of a therapeutic relationship (Lamson, 1986). How exactly do social workers go about establishing such relationships? Over 30 years ago, Carl Rogers identified empathy, respect, and genuineness as being necessary for the therapeutic relationship. When these are communicated to clients along with a non-judgmental attitude and an unconditional acceptance of their individual worth, a relationship begins to develop. Without the social worker engaging the client or building rapport, the client is unlikely to share any personally important information. Patterson (1985) writes, "Counseling or psychotherapy is an interpersonal relationship. Note that I don't say that counseling or psychotherapy *involves* an interpersonal relationship—it *is* an interpersonal relationship" (p. 3).

3. Once the social worker establishes rapport, he or she begins to explore and assess the client's problem. The social worker needs to understand what kind of assistance the client seeks, when the problem began, what factors complicate solving the problem, what efforts have been made, and what resources are available to the client. During this phase, the social worker finds a place to start the problem-solving process. Both client and social worker must agree on and choose some aspect of the problem causing trouble for the client (Moursund, 1985). Often social workers support and encourage clients by providing them with an infusion of hope that their present situation can be improved.

4. When client and social worker reach agreement on what needs to be done and what realistically can be done, a contract is developed. The contract, which can be either written or verbal, provides focus and clarification—it

serves as a reminder of what the client wants to achieve as well as what can be expected from the social worker.

5. Implementation of the intervention or the actions covered in the agreement constitute the middle phase, or what Hepworth and Larsen (1990) call the "heart of the problem-solving process" (p. 33). They point out that "interventions should directly relate to the problems and to the consequent goals that were mutually negotiated with clients and that were derived from accurate assessment" (p. 33).

6. When client and social worker achieve the contract goals, the final step in the problem-solving process follows. This step involves termination of the therapeutic relationship and evaluation of its results. Either the client or the social worker may begin a discussion about termination when some or all of the agreed goals have been achieved. Judgment about the appropriateness of termination is perhaps the easiest when the intervention is time-limited, based on a set number of sessions, or revolves around specific tasks (such as acquiring or extinguishing certain behaviors). Because many factors affect the decision to terminate, clients commonly drop out of therapy or express an interest in termination prior to achieving all of the stated goals. It is often appropriate to indicate that clients can return should they express an interest at some future time.

How Should I Contract with Clients?

We believe that students are generally well advised to contract with their clients. Before we share some ideas about how to develop effective contracts with clients, however, we want briefly to discuss the concept of contract and its importance in social work practice.

The *Social Work Dictionary* (2nd edition) defines a *contract* as a "written, oral, or implied agreement between the client and the social worker as to the goals, methods, timetables, and mutual obligations to be fulfilled during the intervention process." A contract ensures accountability for all parties in performing the tasks essential for the agreed goals. Contracts are not always written; however, more and more social service agencies are moving in that direction.

The importance of a contract with a client follows from basic social work values, particularly client's right to self-determination. Social work is not something done to clients; it is conducted with their cooperative efforts. Clients are expected to identify and rate the priority of their needs. Unless incapacitated, they are in the best position to determine what will be helpful to them (i.e., what courses of action to pursue) and when their needs have been met. Goals cannot be chosen for clients, but result from discussion, clarification, and other social work processes. During the course of intervention, a contract helps both social worker and client stay focused on the purpose of their work together. In addition to stating the agreed goals, the contract will specify the activities or interventions to be used, their frequency, any fees, and other agreements.

The essentials for developing contracts—discussed in Chapter 3—were derived from the SPIRO model (Pfeiffer & Jones, 1972)—which suggests (1) that *specific* goals be written, (2) that these goals be *performance* oriented, (3) that the *involvement* (roles) of the respective parties be stated, (4) that goals be *realistic* (feasible), (5) and that the results of your efforts be *observable* (measurable).

Contracting entails much more than we can tell you in this brief section. A useful article by Barker (1987) contains a contract that he has used with his clients in private practice. (If you need more information on the topic, you are encouraged to consult Epstein, 1980; Fatis & Konewko, 1983; Hepworth & Larsen, 1990; Maluccio & Marlow, 1974; Miller, 1990; Seabury, 1979; or Sheafor, Horejsi, & Horejsi, 1988.)

What Do I Need to Know about Agency Recording?

Recording is an essential part of social work practice. The profession has always emphasized recording for two very important reasons. First, it is assumed that there is an essential connection between good recording and the effectiveness of service. Second, recording is required in all types of practice in varied fields and settings (Timms, 1972). Its importance has been aptly explained by Siporin (1975): "The recording registers significant facts, evidence, judgments, and decisions about the people, problems and situations involved; it defines the reality of the helping situation and experience; presents the quantity and quality of service; and describes and explains the course of helping action" (p. 332).

Recording in social work may take many forms, from process recording—which involves a detailed narrative of all that happened during a client contact—to summary recording and the use of face sheets (intake or admission forms), agency forms, and documents and reports of various kinds. Kagle (1984) has succinctly identified multiple ways that social service records can be used: to assess client and community needs; document services received and the continuity of care; communicate with others providing services to the client; supervise, consult, and educate students and workers; share information with the client; evaluate the process, quality, and impact of service; make administrative decisions; and do research.

Field instructors will orient their student interns to the recording requirements of their agency and will help students to learn how to fill out the various forms according to the breadth and depth of specificity required. Record-keeping can also be a valuable tool in students' own professional growth. Although it would be impossible to prepare students for every type of form that they will encounter on entering a practicum, we can share some general guidelines to help with agency recording.

First of all, keep in mind that the agency record is an official document. It is a permanent register that, while usually confidential, can be subpoenaed as legal evidence. This official record often includes highly personal anecdotes from clients' lives. Kagle (1984) observes, "The client's obligation to share personal information is predicated upon a reciprocal obligation on the part of the social worker and the organization—the obligation not to reveal this information except in specified, socially valued circumstances" (p. 116). This ethical duty is also a legal responsibility. Because of the sensitive nature of this material, confidentiality cannot be stressed enough.

Hepworth and Larsen (1990) provide several general guidelines for maximizing the confidentiality of agency records:

1. Record no more detail than is essential to the function of the agency.
2. Describe clients problems in professional and general terms. Do not incorporate details of intimate matters except where necessary (e.g., a child's description of sexual abuse).
3. Do not include verbatim or process recordings in case files.
4. Do not remove case files from the agency except under extraordinary circumstances and then only with authorization.
5. Do not leave case files open on the desk or out in the open where they might be read by other clients or unauthorized personnel.

If you are in doubt about the amount or level of detail to include in the agency records, then discuss this matter with your field instructor. In some agencies, staff members may keep personal files or notebooks that are not a part of the official files. Your field instructor or faculty field liaison may even require you to keep a journal of your practicum experiences. Many agencies, however, discourage personal notebooks because of the risk that highly sensitive material could be misplaced, lost, or not safeguarded as well as agency files. Therefore, if you want to keep a notebook, ask your field instructor for permission.

If you are permitted to keep personal files or notebooks, you may want to enter in them significant pieces of information about your clients and your impressions, analyses, or hunches. These notebooks contain ideas or insights that may be speculative or considered inappropriate for the official record. Do not allow anyone else to have access to them, and do not keep them longer than absolutely necessary. Also, be sure not to use clients' full names, addresses, or other information that could personally identify them should you lose or misplace your personal notes.

There is much more to recording, and more specifically, to writing up a summary statement of an interview or assessment. *Summary records* are abridgments or abstracts of a client's problem, the services provided to the client, and the client's progress. Agency policy specifies the form and content of such records. Because summary records may be subject to review by a number of people, it is usually good practice to include in them only that which is required and verifiable (Johnson, 1989).

Many agencies rely on the problem-oriented record as a conceptual framework for cataloging essential information. Typically, staff members report both objective and subjective information as well as an assessment and treatment plan for the client. If your agency uses a problem-oriented approach, it is reasonable to expect that this process will be amply explained. However, if you need more explanation of this type of record-keeping, please refer to Appendix A.

What Is Process Recording?

Process recording is a detailed narration of what happened during a social worker's contact with a client. Field instructors and faculty field liaisons sometimes require student interns to do a process recording so that they can examine the dynamics of the client–student interaction. It is an excellent teaching device for learning and refining interviewing and intervention skills. Process recording can help the student to conceptualize and organize ongoing activities with client systems, to clarify the purpose of the interview or intervention, to improve written expression, to identify strengths and weaknesses, and to improve self-awareness (Urbanowski & Dwyer, 1988).

A process recording usually contains

1. names of the worker, client, and others involved in the session; the date of the session;
2. a word-for-word description of what happened (to the extent that it can be recalled);
3. the social worker's observations of client's actions and nonverbal communications;
4. the social worker's assessment of what happened and why;
5. a diagnostic summary that pulls together the social worker's overall thoughts on the entire session (in a paragraph or so); and
6. a brief statement of goals or plans for further contact with the client. (Wilson, 1980)

Dwyer and Urbanowski (1965) suggest the following order for including the major elements in a process recording:

1. purpose of the interview;
2. observations about the physical and emotional climate and its impact on the client;
3. content of the session (actual description of the interview);
4. impressions (but based on facts);
5. social worker's role (a reflection on skills and techniques used); and
6. a plan for future contact and activity.

The actual description of what transpired can be written either as a play script with alternating lines for client and student intern, or as a narrative. When written as a script, the process recording can be used for role-playing in supervisory conferences. In terms of format, Wilson (1981) suggests the use of three or four columns. The first column is for the supervisor's comments and is left blank. The second column is used by the student to describe the content of the interview. The third column is used for recording the student's feelings as the dialogue takes place. Wilson is of the opinion that it is difficult to put one's feelings into writing and that students may tend to use the third column to comment on the client's responses. If that happens, a fourth column should be added to analyze the client's responses. The use of these columns should help the student to develop diagnostic skills by providing a place for recording interpretations while forcing a separation of feelings from professional assessments (Wilson, 1981). Other authors have suggested that the third column be used simply for student reflection (Shulman, 1984).

If you are required to do process recording, you will benefit from the following suggestions:

1. Make sure that the time lag between the interview and writing up the process recording is as short as possible. Since the process recording demands that you describe everything that takes place in the interview, you are likely to forget material with the passage of time.
2. Whenever possible, try to do process recording in conjunction with audio- or video-taping. This will help you to identify significant omissions and to remember things that you might otherwise have forgotten. (Remember to obtain both the client's and agency's permission and be sure that the taping will not unduly inhibit the client or negatively affect the session.)
3. Keep in mind that the purpose of process recording is to help you learn how to be a sensitive, effective practitioner. If you severely edit portions of the interview instead of allowing it to be verbatim, you may be depriving yourself of beneficial feedback.
4. Select the most challenging cases for process recording. Because process recording is a very time-consuming activity, it is very likely that you will be required to do this type of recording on only a few cases. Choose a case that has the greatest potential for learning.
5. Take pains to ensure that your process recording does not jeopardize the client's confidentiality. Use a fictitious name for the client or perhaps only the first letter (Mr. C.). Keep the written records in a secure place. Remember that a process recording is a teaching device only. It should never become a part of the formal record of the agency.

What Should I Keep in Mind When Making a Home Visit?

Social workers make home visits for many different reasons. Whether student interns are observing, visiting a client with another staff person, or conducting their own home visit, they should be clear about the purpose of the visit. The purpose determines how the home visit is arranged, what content is covered during the interview, and what things are carefully observed.

Many home visits are conducted to investigate possible cases of abuse or neglect. After a complaint is issued, social workers go out as quickly as possible. Because they want to see exactly what is happening in the home, in as natural a setting as possible, they may not call ahead. Ideally on an initial investigation, two social workers (or one social worker and a police officer if the situation seems volatile) would visit. When going into unknown situations, an inherent element of danger exists and two persons together provide greater safety (see Chapter 5).

Furthermore, two workers can gather more information than a single social worker. They can divide their effort so that, for example, one speaks to a parent while the other talks to the children. This arrangement allows for less manipulation by the client. Going into a different room or part of the house also allows greater opportunity to observe ventilation, heating, sanitation, and safety hazards within the home.

Clients on investigative home visits are often frightened and intimidated and will perceive you as an authority figure. Clients may be angry about the allegations made against them. Although you can be empathic about their feelings, you are required to explain your job clearly. Try not to be threatening, as you need to lay the groundwork for potential future social work intervention.

If the purpose of the home visit is to offer assistance, then it is almost always best to call ahead and ask clients when you may make a visit. This enables more efficient use of your time—you will not be going places only to find no one at home. Giving notice conveys an attitude of respect for the client's sense of privacy and recognition that the client's time is important and should not be inconveniently interrupted. Many people do not enjoy it when others just show up on their doorstep—particularly people they do not know well. Another advantage of informing these clients ahead of time is that they can gather any necessary papers or documents.

As you enter a home, it is usually a good practice to engage in small talk for a few minutes until the client has a chance to relax a bit. You can thank the client for his or her directions, mention something you saw as you drove or walked to the client's house, or comment on objects you see in the home—photographs of family members, homemade articles, collections that might indicate hobbies, or books or magazines being read.

One of the main advantages of making a home visit is that you can gain a much better understanding of how an individual or a family functions on a daily basis. In a short amount of time you can observe interactions among family members, assess the family's resources, and begin to understand what a day in the life of your client is like.

Almost every student intern is nervous the first time that he or she makes a home visit. With experience, you will feel more and more at ease. One child protection worker recounted his first home visit as follows:

> I felt like a child playing a grown-up's game. How was I going to pull this one off? I remember being so nervous. I walked into the client's home, pulled out a notebook with a long list of questions, and in a very stiff manner began my interrogation. I scarcely lifted my head up to hear the answers. Now, several years later, when I run into my former client we always laugh about that first meeting. She, too, remembers being extremely nervous, so much so that she never realized how uncomfortable I was!

Plan on taking from 45 minutes to an hour for most home visits. If you know you will want to return, then ask when you can come back. Whether you take someone with you on a subsequent visit will depend on how the first visit went.

How Do I Refer a Client to Another Agency or Professional?

As professionals, social workers' commitment to clients demands making the best possible match between clients' needs and the services or resources most likely to meet those needs. A *referral* is the linking of a client with an agency, program, or individual professional who can provide a needed service. A referral to an outside resource may be made at the time of intake, at any time during the ongoing work with a client, or while terminating service with a client. However, student interns are more likely to make referrals as part of the termination plan, since agencies' intake processes are generally shouldered by their most experienced workers.

Many reasons necessitate making a referral. You might identify, for instance, the need for a diagnostic service or consultation to assist with the intervention you will be providing to the client. On other occasions, the referral may demand a collaborative working relationship in which the referring agency coordinates services and retains primary responsibility for the case (Siporin, 1975).

Epstein (1980) lists several of the most common reasons for making a referral:

1. Lack of staff with necessary skills.
2. Lack of sufficient staff.
3. Clients or their problems outside the normal and usual mission or function of the agency.
4. Presumed superiority of the quality of some other agency's resources.
5. Presumed quantity of services available in another agency.
6. Assumption that another agency has been vested with responsibility for certain classes of clients or problems. (p. 155)

Referring clients to other resources requires careful work. Weissman (1976) has reported that within a group of individuals referred to an agency for service, 32 percent had no contact with the agency and another 20 percent had no involvement with the agency after the initial contact. Thus, in over 50 percent of the cases, the purpose of the referral (linking a client with needed resources) had not been served.

The referral process involves several types of interventions and consists of three stages: advising and preparing clients for referral, referring and aiding clients in linkage with needed services, and following up on the referrals.

Generally, when you have identified a need that cannot be met at your agency, you should make a referral to an outside resource. Your first task in this stage is to advise the client of this and to make sure that the client is in agreement. The decision to seek additional help should emerge from your joint deliberation. It may be necessary for you to present information to help the client realize the necessity of the referral. Do not underestimate the resourcefulness of clients. Explore with them resources within their own natural support system (e.g., family, friends, neighbors) as well as other formal community agency resources.

While deciding together what resource would be the best match for the clients' needs, respect the clients' right to self-determination. Encourage clients to express their feelings about seeking additional help elsewhere as well as their feelings about the specific agency or professional being considered. Deal with any doubts, fears, or misconceptions about the resource being discussed. If brochures or pamphlets are available, share these and other information, but be careful not to make promises about what this agency or professional will do.

If the nature of the referral means that a client will have no further dealings with you, and if you sense that the client is feeling a sense of loss or ambivalence about terminating work with you, acknowledge that the time the two of you have spent together has been meaningful. Take pains to prevent the client from feeling that he or she is being rejected or betrayed. Do not sabotage the referral by giving covert messages that no one will be as caring as you are.

In the second stage of the referral process—referring and aiding clients in making the linkage—you will need to estimate the client's ability to make the necessary connections. "Some clients can be given full rein to make a contact and complete the procedures on their own. Some clients need to be carefully rehearsed and escorted" (Siporin, 1975, p. 314).

When possible, use a multipronged approach. For instance, you may have the client schedule the necessary appointment from the phone in your office so that you can be there to assist. You may follow this by making a written request or report, getting the client's permission to share pertinent agency files, or helping the client to complete an application form.

Weissman (1976) suggests use of the following connection techniques:

1. Write out the necessary facts: the name and address of the resource, how to get an appointment, how to reach the resource, and what the client may expect upon arriving there.
2. Provide the client with the name of a specific contact person at the resource.
3. Provide the client with a brief written statement addressed to the resource describing in precise terms the nature of the problem and the services desired by the client. Involve the client in composing the statement.
4. In case the client is apprehensive or diffident about going to the resource alone, arrange for a family member or friend to accompany the client. You may choose to accompany him or her yourself. (p. 52)

The third stage of the referral process consists of following up with the client. Weissman (1976) suggests several ways to go about this. You might ask the client to call you after the initial contact. Or, with the client's permission, you may call the client at a date after the scheduled first contact with the referred resource. Another approach is to plan a session with the client before and immediately after the scheduled appointment with the resource.

Your field instructor needs to assist you particularly when you are making referrals that require a consultation or a collaborative arrangement. At times, your student status may work to a disadvantage because your authority is not equal to that of other professionals with higher status. In such cases Specht (1988) suggests that "if difficulty is expected, the social worker might consider involving the agency's executive director or consulting psychiatrist in making the referral" (p. 181).

How Do I Know If a Client Is Suicidal?

The adult suicide rate in the United States has remained fairly stable over the years. Although in 1985 there were 28,500 deaths attributed to suicide, this figure reflects only known, successful suicides. Kaplan and Sadock (1988) estimate that the number of attempted suicides is eight to ten times larger. The suicide rate for adolescents increased by 136 percent between 1960 and 1980. After accidents and homicides, suicides are the leading cause of death in the 15- to 24-year-old age group (Wodarski & Harris, 1987). Each year, about a half-million young people between the ages of 15 and 24 will attempt suicide. Adults and adolescents with depression are particularly at risk, as are those with serious chronic physical diseases. Several studies have identified factors associated with suicide (Cliffone, 1990; Hepworth, Farley, & Griffiths, 1988; Litman, Faberow, Wold, and Brown, 1974; Tuckman & Youngman, 1968). Persons at high risk for suicide tend to

- live alone (e.g., separated, divorced, or widowed) or feel estranged, isolated;
- have made previous attempts or have a definite plan or available method in mind;
- abuse alcohol or other drugs, are depressed, or have significant irritation or anger (including inability to tolerate small failures);
- have experienced a recent loss (e.g., loss of physical health, job, or significant relationship);
- have intense feelings of hopelessness or anxiety; and
- have relatives or friends who have committed suicide.

Warning signs that may indicate a client is contemplating suicide include

- loss of interest in favorite activities or decline in school achievement;
- sudden withdrawal from family and friends;
- persistent feelings of worthlessness or self-hatred; sadness, moodiness, and sudden tearful reactions (a mood change may occur after suicide has been decided on);
- preoccupation with death themes (e.g., talk of death or dying, even in a "joking" manner);
- giving away possessions and getting affairs in order;
- increased use of drugs and alcohol;
- changes in sleeping or eating patterns (e.g., loss of appetite, arising too early);
- agitation or loss of energy; and
- deterioration in personal habits (e.g., sloppy personal appearance, dirty clothes, messy room) (Lamb, 1990; Hepworth et al., 1988).

Although it may not be unusual for most people to have at least considered the notion of suicide at some time in their lives, healthy individuals do not dwell on these thoughts. You should be concerned any time that a client mentions suicidal ideation. Sometimes these are brief, passing thoughts; at other times they are recurrent and seriously considered notions. However, you should be especially concerned with any client who has several of the characteristics listed above. For example, a client who is clinically depressed, or who has previously attempted suicide, and who has recently experienced a major loss deserves special attention. The more of these characteristics you can identify in your clients, the more concerned you should be.

Suicidal death prediction (lethality) scales have been developed to reflect the different risk factors associated with particular sex and age groupings. If you are in a setting where suicidal calls or threats are fairly frequent, then you may want to obtain such scales as have been developed by Lettieri (1982) and others.

What Do I Do If I Suspect My Client Is Going to Attempt Suicide?

Assuming that you have determined your client to be at high risk for committing suicide because he or she has several of the characteristics listed above or because the client has made a direct or indirect reference to suicidal ideation, your first step will be to ask the client directly if he or she is seriously considering suicide. Look the client in the eye and don't be shy or hesitant—this is a serous matter. If you have a good rapport with the client, generally he or she will be candid. If the client answers in the affirmative, then ask the client to contract with you not to attempt suicide without giving you some more time to help. Attempt to understand the depth of the client's despair. Don't minimize it. At the same time, try to infuse hope. Discuss the progress that the client has made. Point out the client's strengths and positive characteristics. Be optimistic and enthusiastic about what the two of you have accomplished.

If the client admits to planning suicide, or even if the client denies it but you judge the risk of suicide to be severe, you will need to discuss immediate psychiatric hospitalization. If the client does not agree to the hospitalization, inform him or her that in a situation such as this the policy is to inform your agency supervisor, responsible people in the client's life, and possibly the police. Immediately involve your agency supervisor, if possible, while the client is still in your office. You and your supervisor together may then decide to contact a family member, friend, or some other significant person in the client's life. In an emergency such as a suicide attempt, do not worry about breaking client confidentiality. "The duty to save a human life would take precedence over the duty to keep information shared by a client confidential . . ." (Reamer, 1982, p. 584). Depending on the seriousness of the threat, protective actions (e.g., inpatient hospitalization) or involvement of legal authorities may be required even if the client objects.

Additional measures can be taken to manage the suicidal crisis. Ewing (1982) suggests that the client be informed of your availability to be reached by phone. This can be accomplished between agency visits by making telephone "appoint-ments" when the client may call you in your office and talk for a brief period. Inform the client of the availability of emergency psychiatric services and crisis counseling hotlines when you cannot be reached in your office. Although practitioners will sometimes give out their home phone numbers in situations such as this, students generally are advised against this practice. If it is vital that the client reach you at home, then leave your number with the community's 24-hour crisis hotline or the agency's on-call staff members so that they can call you and you can then return the client's call.

Remember that any time you are dealing with a suicidal client or a client you even suspect may be suicidal, you must inform your field instructor.

How Do I Terminate Services with a Client?

Termination means the ending, limiting, or concluding of services. Not much has been written about termination in the helping process in social work literature. Possibly, this is because termination is an aspect of professional practice that resists precise definition (Goldstein, 1973).

Part of the problem in discussing the termination of services with a client comes from not knowing when a client will stop requesting services. Clients may decide not to appear for a scheduled second appointment or the planned final session. Premature and unilateral terminations by clients (i.e., terminations against professional advice) are often thought to represent unresolved resistance. Sensitive areas may have been opened up that the client is uncomfortable handling. This discomfort may result in strong denial or minimization of the problem.

Although students may be personally disappointed or feel that they have failed whenever they experience a premature termination, there are many reasons why clients may prematurely terminate services: the original problem may have actually improved in a short span of time; the client may have moved or be planning to move to another geographic area; there may have been major changes in the client's life (e.g., divorce from an abusing spouse or a prison term for that person). Other changes such as taking a new job, the birth of a child, or a serious illness of a close relative make it difficult for clients to continue with a social service agency. If a student believes that a client needs further help, then the student may gently challenge the client's reasoning behind the decision to terminate, but ultimately must respect the client's wishes. In such instances, it is advised that students inform clients that they can return to the agency if the need arises at some future time.

Termination of services also occurs when social worker and client jointly agree to conclude the service agreement. This may come about whenever either party believes that the client should be referred to another agency (e.g., for detoxification), or to another professional (e.g., a therapist who specializes in working with incest survivors). Termination may also be scheduled because both client and social worker believe that the original goals have been met (i.e., further work is not necessary or desired), because progress is not being made, or because the practitioner is departing (e.g., the semester is ending for the student intern). In addition to premature termination, Hepworth and Larsen (1990) identify four other types of termination:

1. planned terminations determined by temporal constraints;
2. planned terminations with time-limited modalities;

3. planned terminations involving open-ended modalities; and
4. terminations due to the departure of a practitioner.

Schools, hospitals, youth camps, and similar institutions are examples of settings where temporal factors determine when termination will take place. In these settings, there is a reduced possibility that clients will interpret the termination as being arbitrarily imposed and have feelings of desertion or abandonment. The predetermined ending time, however, may not be appropriate for every client, and in such cases students must deal with the feelings (the client's as well as their own) that result from untimely separation. Where necessary, students will make arrangements for their clients to receive additional services.

Planned terminations associated with time-limited modalities involve the client's knowing from the very beginning how long the service will last. This reduces the degree of emotional attachment and dependency, and the feeling of loss that clients may experience as the result of termination. Nevertheless, even in time-limited modalities, clients do form attachments and experience some sense of loss. Student interns must be sensitive to these reactions and allow the client to express these feelings.

In agencies where open-ended modalities of service are used, students need to begin thinking about termination when they start to feel that the gains from continued service will be minor at best. If the client has experienced improvement, but now progress is so slow as to be imperceptible, then the student and the client should discuss this. If both concur that progress has slowed to a halt, then the client's options are (1) to take a furlough from services, (2) to cease services altogether, or (3) to continue with another practitioner.

It is not uncommon for students to feel a little nervous when thinking about termination—especially when a strong working relationship has developed. If the student suggests that his or her assistance is no longer needed, will the client feel rejection? Could a sense of rejection propel the client to regress? Sullivan (1954) has probably added to students' fears by noting that leave-taking, if done badly, can do great damage and that good psychotherapeutic work can be horribly garbled or completely destroyed in the last few minutes (p. 215).

However, many social work practitioners dispute this position. They believe that it overdramatizes the social worker's impact on the client. According to Epstein (1980), "It is a rare client who truly becomes unhappy or adrift when termination occurs" (p. 257). Nevertheless, the ending phase of the helping process is the culmination of all of the energies and efforts previously applied and should be taken seriously. Termination can be conceptualized as a series of discrete tasks, which you can review in order to help plan for the concluding of services with a client:

1. Determine the most appropriate time to conclude services.
2. Anticipate the emotional reactions commonly experienced.
3. Recognize the conflict in being helped and needing to move away from it.
4. Discuss what the client has learned and how the problem-solving experience can be transferred to future problems.

5. Plan for the stabilization of the client's gains and continued growth.
6. Evaluate the service provided and the achievement of goals.
7. Emphasize the agency's continued interest in the client's well-being and suggest that he or she seek help again if needed.

The dynamics of each case will influence the way you actually approach termination with a client. Create in your mind a continuum for each of the concepts of emotional involvement, anxiety over termination, extent of problem resolution, and prognosis for future success. Different points on these continuums will characterize every client, and these positions will affect the way that the client experiences termination.

Many authors have provided guidelines for effective termination. After reading this section, you may wish to consult several of the references at the end of the chapter for additional help with your termination efforts. But first we want to add a few guidelines from Egan (1990):

1. Plan for a termination in the helping process right from the beginning. (This can be accomplished in the client's service agreement or contract by setting an approximate ending date or the expected number of sessions.)
2. Be sensitive to self-indulgent dependency—both the client's and your own. Be alert to cues which suggest that the relationship is becoming more important than the problem management process.
3. State in the contract the degree of progress or change that would be sufficient for termination. End the helping process when it is clear that the goals have been accomplished.

Finally, with some clients who have become overly dependent, it is a good idea to take a gradual approach to termination by lengthening the time between sessions. During this weaning process, make sure that the client is connected with other natural helpers, informal resources, or sources of social support. For clients who are terminating even though significant problems remain, you can suggest follow-up or booster sessions after official termination. Do everything to make a termination as positive an experience for the client as possible and to keep it from being abrupt or unexpected.

IDEAS FOR ENRICHING YOUR PRACTICUM EXPERIENCE

1. Discuss with your field instructor whether a good learning activity for you would be to attend a support group meeting outside of the agency (e.g., Alcoholics Anonymous, Al-Anon). If you do attend, note what preconceived notions are broken as a result.
2. Find out if there are any films, videos, or audiocassettes that the agency has used in the past 3 years to train staff. Ask your field instructor if you may view or listen to these when you have no assigned or scheduled activities (e.g., a client cancels an appointment).

3. If your field instructor or faculty field liaison does not require a process recording or any recording (video or audio) of one of your sessions with a client, then ask if you may do one. Then, as part of supervision, ask your agency supervisor for helpful (constructive) criticism that will make you a more skilled social worker.

4. What is the source of the majority of referrals to your program? What is the profile of the "typical" client? If no such information is available, then ask your field instructor if you may spend some unscheduled time answering these questions from a random sample of 25 closed cases.

5. Browse through the index for this past year and several other years in *Social Work Research and Abstracts*. Look for informative articles on issues, programs, or problems such as those that you commonly encounter in your practicum. Read relevant articles for your professional growth and share them with your field instructor and integrating seminar.

CASE VIGNETTES TO STIMULATE YOUR THINKING

Vignette A

An adolescent who has been having a difficult time with his parents is one of your clients. He is a bright, intelligent 16-year-old who is attractive and personable. You like him a lot and suspect that he is more open with you than he was with his previous social worker. He is rather moody, however, and seems to be very depressed on occasion. Usually by the following week, he has snapped out of his blue funk. Today, he seems more depressed than you have ever seen him. You suspect that he is planning either to run away from home or possibly to commit suicide. When you try to probe, he becomes uncooperative. You ask him to sign a contract agreeing not to commit suicide. He refuses, saying that it is unnecessary. At the end of the appointment, he gets up and says, "Maybe I'll see you next week."

QUESTIONS

Should you inform the adolescent's parents that he is potentially suicidal?

Should you arrange an inpatient hospitalization?

Is it necessary to involve your agency supervisor?

Vignette B

In a new practicum you will be the case manager for five severely mentally ill persons. After a week of orientation and shadowing your agency supervisor, she hands you the files and asks that you contact the clients as soon as possible. With the first case, a 64-year-old woman with a record of seven hospitalizations over the past 5 years, there has been no contact for 3 months.

You try to reach the client by phone, and although it is a working number, no one answers. No one answers when you call again later in the morning and several times in the afternoon. The next day you make about six efforts to reach the client but to no avail. There is no family member or close relative. You decide to make a home visit.

The client lives in a seedy neighborhood where about every third house appears to have a junked and abandoned car in the yard. Wind-blown litter and trash is everywhere. The house where your client lives looks as if it should be condemned. The front porch is sagging badly and several of the floor boards are rotten. You knock on the front door, and for a brief moment you think you hear some movement inside. No one answers the door. You knock again louder, but with the same result.

QUESTIONS

Should you try to peek into one of the windows to see if you can see anyone?
Should you go to the neighbors and ask them what they know about your client?
Should you call the police and ask them to assist you?
Should you return to the agency to confer with your supervisor?

REFERENCES

Bagarozzi, D. A., & Anderson, S. A. (1989). *Personal, marital, and family myths: Theoretical formulations and clinical strategies.* New York: W. W. Norton.

Barker, R. L. (1987). Spelling out the rules and goals: The written worker–client contract. *Journal of Independent Social Work, 1*(2), 67–77.

Brammer, L. M. (1985). *The helping relationship: Process and skills.* Englewood Cliffs, NJ: Prentice-Hall.

Cliffone, J. (1990). Adolescent suicide: A review of possible causal factors and implications for prevention. *School Social Work Journal, 14*(2), 7–17.

Corey, M. S., & Corey, G. (1989). *Becoming a helper.* Pacific Grove, CA: Brooks/Cole.

Cournoyer, B. (1991). *The social work skills workbook.* Belmont, CA: Wadsworth.

Dwyer, M., & Urbanowski, M. (1965, May). Student process recording: A plea for structure. *Social Casework, 46,* 283–286.

Egan, G. (1990). *The skilled helper: A systematic approach to effective helping.* Pacific Grove, CA: Brooks/Cole.

Epstein, L. (1980). *Helping people: The task-centerd approach.* St. Louis: Mosby.

Ewing, C. P. (1982). Crisis intervention: Helping clients in turmoil. In P. A. Keller & L. G. Ritt (Eds.), *Innovations in clinical practice: A source book* (Vol. 1). Sarasota, FL: Professional Resource Exchange.

Fatis, M., & Konewko, P. J. (1983). Written contracts as adjuncts in family therapy. *Social Work, 28*(2), 161–163.

Goldstein, H. (1973). *Social work practice: A unitary approach.* Columbia, SC: University of South Carolina Press.

Hepworth, D. H., Farley, O. W., & Griffiths, J. K. (1988). Clinical work with suicidal adolescents and their families. *Social Casework, 69*(4), 195–203.

Hepworth, D. H., & Larsen, J. A. (1990). *Direct social work practice: Theory and skills.* Belmont, CA: Wadsworth.

Johnson, L. C. (1989). *Social work practice.* Needham Heights, MA: Allyn & Bacon.

Kadushin, A. (1972). *The social work interview.* New York: Columbia University Press.

Kagle, J. D. (1984). *Social work records.* Homewood, IL: Dorsey.

Kaplan, H. I., & Sadock, B. J. (1988). *Synopsis of psychiatry.* Baltimore: Williams & Wilkins.

Lamb, J. M. (1990). The suicidal adolescent: How you can help. *Nursing 90, 20*(5), 72–76.

Lamson, A. (1986). *Guide for the beginning therapist: Relationship between diagnosis and treatment.* New York: Human Sciences Press.

Lettieri, D. J. (1982). Suicidal death prediction scales. In P. A. Keller & L. G. Ritt (Eds.), *Innovations in clinical practice: A source book* (pp. 265–288). Sarasota, FL: Professional Resource Exchange.

Litman, R. E., Faberow, N. L., Wold, C. I., & Brown, T. R. (1974). Prediction models of suicidal behaviors. In H. Beck, L. P. Resnick, & D. J. Lettieri (Eds.), *The prediction of suicide.* Bowie, MD: Charles Press.

Maluccio, A., & Marlow, W. (1974). The case for the contract. *Social Work, 19*(1), 28–36.

Miller, L. J. (1990). The formal treatment contract in the inpatient management of borderline personality disorder. *Hospital and Community Psychiatry, 41*(9), 1009–1012.

Moursund, J. (1985). *The process of counseling and therapy.* Englewood Cliffs, NJ: Prentice-Hall.

Patterson, C. H. (1985). *The therapeutic relationship: Foundations for an electric psychotherapy.* Pacific Grove, CA: Brooks/Cole.

Pfeiffer, J. W., & Jones, J. E. (1972). Criteria of effective goal-setting: The SPIRO model. In *The 1972 annual handbook for group facilitators.* La Jolla, CA: University Associates.

Reamer, F. G. (1982). Conflicts of professional duty in social work. *Social Casework, 63*(10), 579–585.

Rothman, J. (1968). Three models of community organization practice. In *National conference on social welfare, social work practice.* New York: Columbia University Press.

Seabury, B. (1979). Negotiating sound contracts with clients. *Public Welfare, 37*(2), 33–38.

Sheafor, B. W., Horejsi, C. R., & Horejsi, G. A. (1988). *Techniques and guidelines for social work practice.* Boston: Allyn & Bacon.

Shulman, L. (1984). *The skills of helping individuals and groups.* Itasca, IL: F. E. Peacock.

Siporin, M. (1975). *Introduction to social work practice.* New York: Macmillan.

Specht, H. (1988). *New directions for social work practice.* Englewood Cliffs, NJ: Prentice-Hall.

Sullivan, H. S. (1954). *The psychiatric interview.* New York: W. W. Norton.

Timms, N. (1972). *Recording in social work.* London: Routledge & Kegan Paul.

Tuckman, J., Youngman, W. F. (1968). A scale for assessing suicide risk of attempted suicides. *Journal of Clinical Psychology, 24*(1), 17–19.

Urbanowski, M. L., & Dwyer, M. M. (1988). *Learning through field instruction.* Milwaukee, WI: Family Service of America.

Weissman, A. (1976, January). Industrial social services: Linkage technology. *Social Casework, 57,* 5–57.

Wilson, S. (1980). *Recording: Guidelines for social workers.* New York: Free Press.

———. (1981). *Field instruction: Techniques for supervisors.* New York: Free Press.

Wodarski, J. S., & Harris, P. (1987). Adolescent suicide: A review of influences and the means for prevention. *Social Work, 32*(6), 477–483.

ADDITIONAL READINGS

Amidei, N. (1982, Summer). How to be an advocate in bad times. *Public Welfare,* pp. 37–42.

Baldwin, M., & Satir, V. (Eds.). (1987). *The use of self in therapy.* New York: Haworth.

Compton, B. R., & Galaway, B. (1989). *Social work processes.* Belmont, CA: Wadsworth.

Cormier, W. H., & Cormier, L. S. (1985). *Interviewing strategies for helpers.* Pacific Grove, CA: Brooks/Cole.

Dear, R. B., & Patti, R. J. (1981). Legislative advocacy: Seven effective tactics. *Social Work, 26*(4), 289–296.

Eggert, G. M., Friedman, B., & Zimmer, J. G. (1990). *Journal of Gerontological Social Work, 15*(3/4), 75–101.

Evans, D. R., Hearn, M. T., Uhlemann, M. R., & Ivey, A. E. (1984). *Essential interviewing: A programmed approach to effective communication.* Pacific Grove, CA: Brooks/Cole.

Fortune, A., Pearlingi, B., & Rochelle, C. D. (1992). Reactions to termination of individual treatment. *Social Work, 37*(2), 171–178.

Frederick, C. J. (1983). *Suicide prevention procedures.* In P. A. Keller & L. G. Ritt (Eds.), *Innovations in clinical practice: A source book* (Vol. 2, pp. 161–173). Sarasota, FL: Professional Resource Exchange.

Garrett, A. M. (1982). *Interviewing: its principles and methods.* New York: Family Service Association of America.

Kutchins, H. (1991). The fiduciary relationship: The legal basis for social workers' responsibilities to clients. *Social Work, 36*(2), 106–113.

Lurie, A., Pinsky, S., Rock, B., & Tuzman, L. (1989). The training and supervision of social work students for effective advocacy practice: A macro system perspective. *The Clinical Supervisor, 7*(2/3), 149–158.

Okun, B. F. (1987). *Effective helping: Interviewing and counseling techniques.* Pacific Grove, CA: Brooks/Cole.

Parad, H. J., & Parad, L. G. (1991). *Crisis intervention: The practitioner's sourcebook for brief therapy.* Milwaukee: Family Service America.

Reamer, F. G. (1982). *Ethical dilemmas in social services.* New York: Columbia University Press.

Schubert, M. (1982). *Interviewing in social work practice: An introduction.* New York: Council on Social Work Education.

Sosin, M., & Calum, S. (1983). Advocacy: A conceptualization for social work practice. *Social Work, 28*(1), 12–17.

Specht, H., & Specht, R. (1986). Social work assessment: Route to clienthood. *Social Casework, 67*(10), 587–593.

Super, S. I. (1982, Summer). Successful transition: Therapeutic interventions with the transferred client. *Clinical Social Work Journal, 10,* 113–122.

Timms, N. (1972). *Recording in social work.* London: Routledge & Kegan Paul.

Weber, T. (1985). A beginner's guide to the problem-oriented first family interview. *Family Process, 24*(3), 357–364.

Woods, M. E., & Hollis, F. (1990). *Casework: A psychosocial therapy.* New York: McGraw-Hill.

CHAPTER 7

Pragmatic Concerns

Overview

This chapter contains practical advice regarding miscellaneous situations or questions that may arise during the social work practicum.

What Do I Do If I Get Sick or Am Running Late and Miss My Appointments?

It is probably inevitable that at some time during a practicum you will become ill, have car trouble, or experience another problem that may cause you to miss some scheduled appointments. Once you know that you will be delayed or will miss an appointment, the professional course of action is to call the agency. Ask the secretary to contact your clients, your agency supervisor, and other involved parties to inform them of your absence. If you have an infectious illness (e.g., the flu), then it is much kinder to miss an appointment or two than to infect co-workers and clients. Appointments can be rescheduled when you are feeling better. If you are too ill to go to work, do not feel obligated to contact clients from home and provide routine counseling over the phone. If your car breaks down, and there is no phone close by, all you can do is to call the agency at the first opportunity. Once you are back in the agency, reschedule all missed appointments as soon as possible.

Will I Be Asked to Share a Desk or Office?

Student interns do not always find that they have their own private office in the practicum agency. Often, they may share an office with another student or students. Ideally, however, students should have their own desks and phones.

When an office is shared with others (and it may be the field instructor), the important thing to keep in mind is consideration for others.

If you use a desk that is shared with another student or staff person, keep it tidy. Ensure that the working surface of the desk is clean before you leave each day. If you share an office, try not to monopolize it or the phone with loud conversation when your office-mate is working. Do not transform the office into your personal habitat. It is probably best if you do not bring in radios, televisions, or expensive personal effects to entertain you or to decorate the office.

If you share an office and you need private space for counseling, then the agency should have a vacant office for either you or your office-mate to use temporarily. Sometimes this space must be scheduled in advance. Be sure to learn the procedures for this before you find yourself with a client and no space suitable for interviewing or counseling. If the agency is critically short of space and on more than one occasion you and a client have to use an unsuitable area (such as a vacant corner of the waiting room), then report this to your faculty field liaison. The agency may not be well suited for the training of students. It is especially critical that the space or rooms utilized for working with clients not jeopardize their confidentiality by others overhearing or observing emotional responses.

What Do I Do If I Am Given Too Much or Too Little Responsibility?

Too much responsibility can be frightening! Overwhelming! A couple of years ago a student confided that in her placement, interns were assigned six or more cases the first day after orientation and told to schedule the appointments. They were expected to handle themselves as professionals, and if they needed help to ask for it. No help was given unless it was sought. Although the student's initial reaction was "poor me," by the end of her two semesters there she had been asked to remain as a paid employee. If, however, you feel as though you are being given too much to do, then you probably need to talk to someone. If you suspect that your field instructor will be unsympathetic, then talk with your faculty field liaison.

If you are mildly concerned about what you perceive to be your unproven ability to help others, this probably would not be seen as a serious problem. On the other hand, if you are experiencing tremendous stress (e.g., insomnia, indigestion, panic attacks), then you very likely are being given more responsibility than you can handle. In this instance, it is appropriate to inform your field instructor of what you are feeling or experiencing.

The problem of being given too little responsibility was addressed in Chapter 4. Briefly, students should expect to be occupied in direct service at least half of the time that they are in their placement. If this is not happening, talk first with the field instructor. If additional responsibilities are not given, then share your concerns with the faculty field liaison. All three participants in the learning contract (the student, the faculty field liaison, and the field instructor) need to be involved should problems arise in the practicum. Don't feel that you have to solve major problems in your field instruction by yourself.

Do I Need Liability Insurance?

The United States is a very litigious society. Although the chances of a social work student being sued are small, the expense of defending against even a preposterous charge can quickly go beyond the resources of most students. Having liability insurance does not protect you from being sued. However, if you are sued, the insurance will be greatly appreciated.

Only a few social work programs provide liability insurance for students. Some programs require their students to purchase this insurance. In most programs, students have the option of purchasing liability insurance. Should you buy liability insurance if it is not required? The best argument for buying the insurance is that the National Association of Social Workers Insurance Trust offers it at a relatively inexpensive rate.

Another argument for purchasing the insurance would be if you are placed in an agency where there have been recent suits against staff members or where you feel that conditions are right for a suit against an employee or the agency. On the other hand, you may be provided some protection by the agency's or even the university's liability policy. However, you can't always count on this. You can be sued as an individual. Protection that you think you have under the agency's policy might evaporate if attorneys for the agency point out that you were not a bona fide employee. If you can spare the cash, purchasing liability insurance is not a bad idea, even though it is unlikely that you will ever use it.

May I Audio- or Video-tape Clients?

As part of your course work it may be required or desirable to reproduce one of your sessions with a client. If this requirement comes from your faculty field liaison or another faculty member, don't assume that your agency supervisor will know about it. Discuss your need to audio- or video-tape a client with your agency supervisor. The two of you can then begin the necessary planning and client selection. Keep in mind, though, that it is *always* necessary to obtain the client's permission before you begin to audio- or video-tape—even if the client's identify will not be known to your audience or identifiable characteristics can be obscured in an editing process. Most agencies require that clients indicate their agreement to taping by signing a written release or consent form. This is a good idea even if the agency does not have a prepared form. When you are interested in taping children, obtain permission from their parents or guardians.

Once permission has been secured, it is a good idea to test the equipment and make sure that you know how to operate the video or audio recorders. Experiment with the placement of the microphone or camera to ensure that you get the best possible recording. Have everything arranged so that there will be minimal distraction or attention given to the equipment once the clients arrive. Do not remind clients to look toward the camera. Try to keep the equipment as unobtrusive as possible. Remember, the process of recording should be less important than what you and your clients achieve together in the session.

May I Accept A Gift from a Client?

Sometimes clients are so appreciative that they want to give their favorite social worker a gift. Some agencies have policies on receiving gifts; others do not. Check with your agency supervisor if a client hints that he or she will be bringing you a present. The client's giving of a small gift may be a demonstration of simple gratitude for being helpful or for simply accepting something that the client said or did. But the gift may also be an attempt to ask the therapist to like the client more, or to manipulate the therapist (Gabel, Oster, & Pfeffer, 1988). This would be particularly the case with expensive or extravagant gifts. In the absence of an agency policy, you may want to devise one of your own—such as not accepting gifts valued at more than 10 dollars. Generally, small tokens of appreciation, such as cookies, a small painting, or a ceramic creation made by the client, can be graciously accepted.

Once in a while, a client will want to give a special student a gift even after a case has been transferred or closed. Generally when this happens, there is some dependency on the client's part and the client may be trying to keep the student involved in the case. In such instances, you may want to have the client leave the gift at the agency or with another worker, so that you can pick it up without becoming entangled again.

Is It Ever Permissible to Date Clients or Co-workers?

Students should not date clients, and as a general rule, should not socialize with clients outside of the agency. Although one date may not lead to romantic involvement, in any dating situation where there is physical attraction the potential for sexual involvement exists. And, it is never permissible for helping professionals to engage in sexual activities with their clients. The NASW Code of Ethics states, "The social worker should under no circumstances engage in sexual activities with clients." In fact, because of its destructive consequences for clients, all of the major mental health professions have explicit prohibitions against therapist–client sexual involvement. In some states legislation has been passed making therapist–client sexual intimacy a criminal offense (Pope, 1986).

If you find that you are strongly attracted to a client, the advised course of action is to speak to your agency supervisor about arranging a transfer of this client to another staff member. Romantic involvement jeopardizes professional objectivity. The therapist's judgment about what is best for the client may be clouded as the therapist becomes overprotective and overinvolved.

One authority advises, "Confine relationships with patients to the office, except for certain specific treatment indications" (Pope, 1978). When would it be appropriate to see a client outside of the office? An example would be when it is impossible to talk or hear in your office (e.g., because of remodeling or construction), and it is convenient to walk to the corner restaurant and talk over coffee or a soft drink. In such instances, inform at least one other person in the agency (e.g., your agency supervisor) of your whereabouts. Although it is clear that, given a choice, some clients may prefer not to meet in the office, the use of an office within an established agency lends an air of propriety. Requests from clients to meet outside of the office may indicate an interest in manipulating or undercutting progress being made in therapy.

It also is not a good idea to date staff members within the agency as long as you are a student there. If the other staff person has supervisory authority over you, dating him or her would be even more ill advised. When there are break-ups, relationships have a way of causing hard feelings. Supervisors could turn vindictive or uncooperative. Even if the relationship weren't to go sour, you might not be able to maximize your learning in an agency where your relationship becomes a prime topic of conversation. (Intra-office relationships are extremely difficult to keep secret.)

Should I Share Personal Information with Clients?

In an effort to understand and relate to you, clients may ask personal questions such as, "Are you married?" "Do you have children?" "How old are you?" or, "How much do they pay you to do this?" If the student can share the information without feeling an invasion of privacy, then it is okay to answer such questions. Schubert (1982) advises answering in a brief and straightforward manner without comment about the meaning of the question. Such questions may be simple social curiosity. Sometimes, however, it is preferable to be a little vague in answering. In response to a question about his or her age, a student might reply, "I'm thirtyish."

Clients may ask about your experience because of a genuine interest in the helper's qualifications. Some clients may be reassured to know that you have completed courses in child development or that you will be completing your degree next year. Do not overexplain or become defensive. The client has a right to decide whether to continue with you or to ask for someone else. If you feel that the client is troubled by your lack of experience, Schubert (1982) suggests that you ask, "Are you afraid that I won't be able to help you?" or, "Does this bother you?" Most clients will be so appreciative of someone assigned to help them that your qualifications will not be a major issue.

If you feel that a client's questions are a little too intrusive, you can deflect them by asking, "Why is that important to you?" or, "How does that relate to your purpose in coming here?" Generally, this will help clients to refocus on what they have come to the agency to obtain or accomplish.

Even though you may see no harm in answering a question about where you live, never give out your address or home phone number to clients without the knowledge of the field instructor. More than one student has been surprised when infatuated or disturbed clients have made unwanted and unanticipated visits to their apartments or homes. Also, nuisance phone calls are always a possibility when you give out your home phone number. Clients who may be suicidal or who may need to reach you in another emergency can call the agency's after-hours number, or you can direct them to call a 24-hour crisis counseling center until you can be reached again at the agency. (In extreme situations, the 24-hour crisis counseling center could be given your home phone number so that they could inform you when a client is having problems. You could return the client's call without the client learning of your home phone number.)

Similarly, it is not advisable to correspond with active or former clients without your agency supervisor's knowledge, even if the clients are incarcerated and in another state. Although you may wish to correspond with a favorite client or an inmate out of concern or friendship, these situations can get out of hand if they are misinterpreted. Someone sitting in a jail cell all day with little to occupy his or her time may build elaborate fantasies and begin to see you in a way you had not intended. This may serve a useful purpose for them, but it can also be quite disconcerting for you when they are released from prison or they unexpectedly travel a long distance to spend some time with you.

How Do I Handle Sexual Harassment?

Sexual harassment is unwanted verbal or physical conduct of a sexual nature. This includes compliments of a very personal or sexual nature, pressure for dates or sexual contact, jokes with suggestive themes, unwelcome notes, or physical activities such as touching, brushing against, unsolicited back rubs, or blocking passage with one's body. The few studies available on sexual harassment of social workers have shown that human service agencies are not immune from this problem and that almost 30 percent of social workers have experienced some form of sexual harassment.

When does a hug or a touch become sexual harassment? Sexual harassment is one sided—there is no reciprocity involved. James (1981) states that the offender's behavior is unwelcome and is almost always repetitive. A single incident usually is not sexual harassment unless a serious threat or assault is involved.

Another aspect of sexual harassment is that the offender may use clout or power of position to insinuate that the victim has much to lose by not going along with the offender's requests. Sexual harassment exists when you fear a loss of position or status, or negative evaluation, because you rejected sexual advances. Both men and women can be victims of sexual harassment.

If you feel that you are being subjected to sexual harassment, you should immediately inform your primary supervisor. If the person harassing you is the supervisor, or if you don't feel comfortable discussing the matter with this person, then by all means contact your faculty field liaison. Often, the situation will not improve until someone—the victim—decides to take a stand. One of our graduate students, placed in a psychiatric setting, was repeatedly subjected to derogatory comments from a male physician about the nature of her work. These comments were completely unfounded and sexist in nature. When the student discussed this situation with her field instructor, a great deal of support was generated for her, and the result was that a letter of disciplinary action was placed in the physician's personnel folder.

Don't be silent just because you are a student or because you don't have much longer in the placement. If you are feeling sexually harassed, it is likely that the same offender has or is harassing others. There are laws to protect you against sexual harassment. Don't be a silent victim. One way to avoid becoming a victim is to familiarize yourself with your agency's policies for complying with sexual harassment laws. Dhooper, Huff, and Schultz (1989) found that 54 percent of social workers surveyed were ignorant of the applicable laws.

What Do I Do When Things Aren't Going Well?

If agencies can be personified as people we know, some would be dynamic—fast moving, attractive, decisive. Others would have a frumpy appearance and would be slow moving and ponderous. Not every student can be placed in a dynamic agency. For one thing, there are probably too few of them and too many students. You know this intellectually and yet you are unhappy in your placement. When should you ask for another placement? Here are some suggested guidelines:

- when you are not getting adequate supervision (and you have repeatedly sought and requested supervision);
- when you are not being given anything to do, or when the work being given to you is clerical and you have made numerous requests for additional responsibility;
- when you are being harassed or feel in danger;
- when you discover that you cannot be empathic with persons you are assigned to counsel because of personal or traumatic experiences with this problem (e.g., you were a victim of child sexual abuse);
- when you are required to be in the agency at a time when you are expected to be in class or at a field seminar, and the agency is inflexible in its demands;
- when there is a significant personality clash between you and your agency supervisor (e.g., the supervisor gives the impression that you can do nothing right and that your work cannot be trusted); or
- when unethical or illegal practices are common occurrences.

Asking for another placement is not a decision to be taken lightly. This is especially true after you have spent 4 or 5 weeks in an agency. Several social work programs allow the student only one "replacement" in another setting. Nonetheless, some problems are so serious that students really ought to seek a new assignment—even if it means losing credit for the month spent in the first agency. Keep in mind, though, that it is not uncommon for students to experience a slow start—for field instructors to give very few assignments the first few weeks until they get to know the student and the student's capabilities. Sometimes the student feels that the first several weeks of a placement are spent reading with very little client contact.

There are logical explanations for this. Supervisors may want students to become more knowledgeable in a given area (e.g., the disease model of alcoholism) and may request completion of specific readings or observations before they assign clients in need of treatment in that area. Or supervisors may want to screen clients to ensure that the student is matched with one who can realistically show progress by the semester's end. Also, they may want to avoid assigning overly complicated cases to a student. Supervisors may want to wait for the right family before involving the student as a co-therapist. Furthermore, students may have to wait for sufficient clients to be recruited or identified before they can become involved as a group leader or co-leader. Often it happens that little in the way of actual planning or recruiting for a new group really occurs until the student is established in the agency. So, expect some delays. Although it is frustrating, your agency supervisor will not always be available on a moment's notice. But none of these situations are by themselves good reasons for changing a practicum.

More serious concerns are when the agency is seriously mismanaged or understaffed, or when unethical practices are tolerated. In our program, a student interning in a group home for adolescents was made responsible for helping the residents prepare their meals over the weekend, but the only food left for her was a single can of lasagna. This event by itself was insufficient reason to remove a student, but it had been preceded by other indications of poor management. Hearing the student's account of this experience and then learning that the police were investigating one staff member for an illegal practice convinced us that the student would not have the type of experience that we had hoped. We moved the student to another agency.

Students should advocate for themselves—to try to rectify unhappy situations to the best of their abilities. When sincere (and usually repeated) effort has been made, then it is up to the faculty field liaison to decide the next course of action. Do not decide to leave an assignment without the approval of the faculty member who placed you there—this could result in a failing grade. What may seem to be an insurmountable problem to a student often turns out to be resolvable when a conscientious faculty member becomes involved.

If you spent a semester in a lackluster agency, or had a field instructor who contributed very little to your educational experience, one way to feel better about this would be to discuss with your faculty field liaison the development or adoption of a student feedback form for field instructors, if one isn't already being used in your program. Examples of such a form can be found in Johnston, Rooney, and Reitmeir (1991), and Fortune et al. (1985). Feedback from students can improve the supervision and quality of future students' learning experiences by documenting when a particular field instructor performs unsatisfactorily.

How Do I Keep Track of Time in the Practicum?

You can keep track of the amount of time spent in your practicum placement by one of many methods. It may be simple enough to remember that you spend all day on Tuesdays and Thursdays and half of each Friday—for a total of 20 hours each week. Such a crude accounting system does not provide any description of *how* you spent your time. If asked about your major activities last week, would you be able to recall them without the aid of some notes? It is important to keep a record of the hours you spend in an agency as well as the variety of experiences to which you are exposed. Reviewing this record from time to time can help you and your agency supervisor to monitor your progress toward your learning objectives and your development as a social worker.

A convenient way to determine what you have been learning in the agency is to review how you have spent your time. Agencies and social work programs use different procedures and forms to keep track of students' use of time. If, however, none is mandated and you are looking for a quick reporting scheme, see Figure 7.1 for an illustration of one (modified from Cooper, 1982) that you could create for your own use.

FIGURE 7.1   Practicum Reporting Form

SOURCE: Adapted from Cooper, W. E. (1982). Time management techniques for clinicians. In P. A. Keller & L. G. Ritt (Eds.), *Innovations in clinical practice: A source book.* Sarasota, FL: Professional Resource Exchange.

Date _____

Student's Name _____   Agency _____

Hours Interned this Week _____   Cumulative Hours _____

Hour	Monday	Wednesday	Friday
8:00 8:30	Team meeting	Supervision with Field Instructor	Agency Research Project (Cont.)
9:00 9:30	Counseling Mrs. J	Staff Inservice	Preparation for Case Presentation
10:00 10:30	Writing Progress Notes and Treatment Plan		Counseling Mr. M
11:00 11:30	Preparation for Afternoon Group		Interview Children's Services Coordinator
12:00 12:30	Lunch	Lunch	Lunch
1:00 1:30	Observation Marital Therapy	Intake Desk	Staffing Crisis Phone Line
2:00 2:30	Counseling Jim C.	Intake Desk	Staffing Crisis Phone Line
3:00 3:30	Writing Progress Notes and Reading on Tourette's	Counseling Ms. W.	Emergency Room Visit
4:00 4:30	Self-Esteem Group Session (6 Kids)	Agency Research Project (Reviewing Files)	Consultation with Jim C.'s Teacher
5:00			

Am I Permitted to Accumulate Overtime or Compensatory Time?

There may be occasions when you will be asked to work days or evenings beyond your scheduled time in the agency. The agency may experience a temporary staff shortage because of illness, vacations, or some other emergency. If you find yourself a few hours ahead in terms of the work time you should have accumulated to that point, it would be appropriate to discuss with your field instructor whether to count these hours toward an earlier ending date for your practicum or whether you could be excused from one of your scheduled days in the agency.

It is not unusual for students to accumulate more hours in the practicum agency than they are required by their social work program. (Usually it indicates that an agency trusts and values a conscientious student.) However, you should not plan to apply any excess hours in this semester's placement toward next semester's practicum. Although this might be allowed by some faculty field liaisons, it certainly is not an entitlement. You can see how the situation could get out of hand—especially if you changed agencies in the second practicum after accumulating 40 extra hours in the first practicum that you wanted to apply to the next agency. If you find yourself acquiring an excessive number of hours in your practicum, discuss this as soon as possible with your faculty field liaison.

How Do I Learn to Leave My Work at the Agency?

For your own mental health and well-being, do not bring client and agency problems home with you. Concern yourself with clients' problems only when you are on duty at the agency. When you are at home or in the classroom, you need to give your attention to your family, friends, or schoolwork. Although it sounds a little callous, it is sometimes helpful to realize that you do not own your clients' problems. You cannot "make" anyone get better. Even though you will do your best to help, clients' problems are *their* problems. If you find yourself not sleeping or being preoccupied with a client's difficulties when you are at home or school, then you are probably overinvolved and are attempting to own the problem. (Some clients will gladly let you own their problems.) If you recognize that you are overinvolved, discuss this with your field instructor or faculty field liaison.

It will not always be easy to leave client problems at the agency at the end of the day. If you weren't concerned about people, you probably wouldn't have chosen the career of social work. However, separating your nonwork life is a mental discipline that you must practice. To help you with this, make a personal rule to not bring paperwork from the agency home with you. Although it might be tempting to catch up on your progress notes or other work-related assignments at home, this is not advised. To do this type of work, client files or charts are usually needed, and students should never take agency files or confidential material out of the office without permission of the agency supervisor or field instructor. In one horror story, a student took several files home one evening only to have her briefcase (which contained the files) stolen from her car. In another, a physician was taking home medical files, and the files actually blew out the window of his car and across the interstate highway.

What Do I Do When I Am Depressed or Have a "Down" Day?

Sometimes the severity of clients' problems (e.g., child sexual abuse, adolescent suicide attempts, domestic violence) can cause students to experience "down" days—especially when a favorite client takes a turn for the worst (e.g., attempts suicide again or gets rearrested). Although intellectually students can tell themselves that it will be impossible to help every client, they are still likely to feel some pain when clients make bad choices for themselves.

It is important for you not to become depressed because of an action that a client freely chose. Do not label yourself as a failure if a client engages in dysfunctioning. Almost always, clients have some problems in everyday functioning or they would not be requesting services from a social service agency. With problems such as substance abuse, it is expected that clients will "fall off the wagon" on one or more occasions even though they may later successfully maintain a life of sobriety. One therapist's technique for avoiding depression when his clients had relapses was to think about the clients' strengths and then envision them using these assets at some future time to live successfully.

If you find yourself more than a little depressed or depressed fairly frequently because of the cases you have been assigned, tell your faculty field liaison. You may need therapy—particularly if these cases are very close to some trauma you have personally experienced. If you find it too difficult to handle the emotional pain shared and experienced in the practicum setting, then you may be better suited for research or administrative social work than direct practice with clients.

What Do I Do if I Overhear Something That Is Illegal or Unethical?

It is possible that you will observe or overhear something in an agency that strikes you as illegal or unethical. Consider this example: A student intern observes a social worker taking a large roll of adhesive tape out of the supply room and putting it into his briefcase to take home. Should the student report this to her field instructor? Probably not. The social worker may be working at home on agency related work and intend to bring the tape back to the office the next morning. Or, he may have absentmindedly put the tape into his briefcase at the end of the day instead of taking it back to his office. Perhaps he will discover his error when he gets home.

However, if you were to observe someone in the agency taking money from clients and promising them extra benefits, misappropriating client funds (e.g., not buying them clothing as promised but spending it on dinner), or kissing a minor client in the office after hours, then you might have a responsibility to report these much more serious accusations to your field instructor.

Sometimes it is very difficult to know whether some action should be reported. One student was told not to use the agency phone for personal calls, yet observed a staff member who tied up a phone line for 45 minutes on a call to her boyfriend. This was not fair, and the student wanted to complain to her field instructor. In fact, she did complain. The field instructor took no action.

The staff member was a personal friend of the field instructor and there was no disciplinary action. But the student was viewed as a malcontent who was always complaining. Her final evaluation was much lower than her midterm evaluation.

The best advice is to consider the seriousness of the offense or charge. Is someone harmed or likely to be harmed? Contemplate what the consequences would be if you are wrong. What if you were mistaken and the 45 minute call was not to a boyfriend but to a legitimate client who was falling apart and needed 45 minutes of the social worker's time? What if the minor that the social worker was kissing was his daughter or niece, and his wife was also sitting in the office out of your line of sight? What if the social worker really did buy clothes with the clients' money and was just teasing you by pretending that he blew the money on dinner? If you are sure that you are right and the charge is serious enough to be unethical, illegal, or unprofessional, then discuss the incident in private with your field instructor or your faculty field liaison, and the two of you can decide what the next step should be.

How Do I Handle Agency Secrets?

Once in a while students learn of transactions or behaviors within an agency that are not common knowledge. For instance, the treasurer may have embezzled a sum of money or the director may have been sued for palimony. Because the agency is not your client, you are not obligated to keep this information confidential in the same way as you have to safeguard sensitive material that clients share with you. However, you would be well advised to be very discreet in revealing these agency secrets.

For one thing, the allegations could turn out to be completely false and the result of vicious rumor. It would be embarrassing (if not irresponsible) if you were to spread such gossip throughout the community. Could you be guilty of slander in this situation? Furthermore, the personal affairs of agency officials may not interfere with their administrative abilities within the agency. Airing an agency's secrets in public could contribute to the agency's loss of reputation in the community and do a disservice to the many fine, hard-working, and unselfish staff members.

If you feel that the private information that you have about the agency has or could have a direct effect on the quality of services to clients or the learning in your practicum, then report this information to either your field instructor or your faculty field liaison. Also report this information if you think it might prevent future students from being placed in the agency. Otherwise, whom you tell about the agency's secrets depends on your own discretion.

How Do I Plan for My Next Practicum?

If you find yourself in a setting where your learning opportunities have been severely limited and you strongly feel that you need another practicum placement in a similar agency, then discuss this with your faculty field liaison. It would be to your advantage to give some thought to the areas of deficiency in this particular practicum setting and to the type of agency or program that could help you to develop needed skills. At some point in your practicum, you may learn of highly recommended agencies or field instructors from students who are farther along in the program than you are. Advocate for yourself sufficiently ahead of time so that your faculty field liaison can assign you to these agencies or with these field instructors.

Occasionally a student will discover that a friend or former fellow student has now obtained a position in an agency and would be willing to supervise the student. As a rule, students should avoid seeking placements where friends, neighbors, family members, or others who would be less than objective would provide supervision. Asking someone with whom you have a strong relationship or tie to supervise you would not be approved by your faculty field liaison and could get you into trouble if discovered later. For you to optimize your learning and grow professionally, it is necessary that your agency supervisor's objectivity not be impaired.

Am I Cut Out for Social Work?

From time to time most professionals wonder if they have chosen the right vocation. That's okay. What you have going for you is that seldom does anyone have to make an immediate decision about a career choice. If your first practicum did not go well, this may not be a reflection on you. Perhaps your supervisor was too often unavailable or too critical. Maybe staff members just didn't reach out to you because of internal strife and poor morale within the agency (e.g., frustration over lack of a pay raise or dissatisfaction with the actions of an executive director). Despite your faculty field liaison's efforts, maybe your experience was not a pleasant one. Don't take this personally. Especially if you are not at the end of your social work program, you will likely have other practicums to test whether social work is a career for you.

Sometimes even a relatively unpleasant practicum yields useful learning about yourself or a certain population of clients. For instance, if you tend to be very trusting of people, you may have learned not to display that trait to drug addicts who are not very far along in their recovery process. Maybe this experience will direct you to another population (e.g., hospice patients) with whom you will build excellent rapport because of the same trait.

Remember: The purpose of the practicum is to provide you with some training experiences; you are a student; and you are not expected to know all of the answers. As far as that goes, even your field instructor or faculty field liaison will not have all of the answers. You don't necessarily have to consider changing careers if you made a few mistakes in your practicum. (Of course, if these were serious mistakes, and you made several of them, this is a different matter.) Sometimes talking with your adviser or your faculty field liaison can help you to think about the advantages and disadvantages of changing majors or careers. Allow yourself the freedom to be a student. If you have a tendency to be overly critical of yourself, then you will not be objective in comparing your progress with that of other students.

Finally, if you felt that you did good work with your clients, be reassured by that. We don't always get recognized for a job well done. In fact, you are more likely to get recognition if you create a serious problem than if you handled your assignments effectively and efficiently. Of course, good work often is noticed and rewarded.

IDEAS FOR ENRICHING YOUR PRACTICUM EXPERIENCE

1. Begin to reflect back on your experience thus far in the practicum. What would you say is the most important thing that you learned from working with the clients? What is the most important thing that you learned from working with staff members? Did you accomplish everything that you set out to learn in your learning contract? What do you still need to learn in the next practicum?

2. Consider what you have learned from this practicum and this academic term and then review your curriculum vitae. What might you change in the way you describe or present yourself?

3. Overall, how would you evaluate the agency and the program to which you were assigned? Would you highly recommend it to other students? During your integrative seminar ask if students can discuss the merits of the agencies where they have spent the past academic term.

4. Ask your field instructor if there are any other similar programs in the community. If there are, seek permission to schedule a visit to learn how they provide services. Do they use the same intake procedures or different ones? Do they provide intervention about the same way as your agency does? Have they conducted any evaluative research on the effectiveness of their program?

CASE VIGNETTES TO STIMULATE YOUR THINKING

Vignette A
Your car is undependable, and it is particularly difficult to start in the morning after it has been idle for 8 or 10 hours. You have taken the car to numerous repair shops, but no one can find the problem. You can't afford to buy a new car at this time, and public transportation is not available within a reasonable walking distance of you.

Since beginning your practicum, problems with starting your car have made you late on three occasions. Once you were only 20 minutes late. The second time you were about 45 minutes late. On the third occasion, your agency supervisor sternly advised you to find another means of transportation because she had to see your client for you. After 4 frustrating weeks, you have just learned that your supervisor lives just a little over a mile from your apartment.

QUESTIONS

Should you ask if you can car pool with your agency supervisor?
What other options are available to you?

Vignette B
For your first practicum you are assigned to a residential facility for persons with developmental disabilities and mental retardation. After the 2nd week, a friend stops by, and since you are not busy at the time, you take about 15 minutes to give your friend a tour of the facility. Later, the agency director makes it clear that you are not to invite friends and family members to the facility. You explain that you had not invited your friend but she had just shown up, and you were merely being polite. Your feelings are a little hurt.

· The next weekend, the interior of the facility is being painted and all but about four clients go home for a visit. Jim, a long-time employee of the facility, has a visit from his girlfriend on Saturday afternoon. They go into the office and keep the door closed for about 2 hours. During this time Jim does not answer the phone or attend to any agency business that you can observe.

QUESTIONS

Should you inform your agency supervisor of Jim's activities?

Should you let Jim know that you felt that he was violating the rules?

Should you cover for Jim?

REFERENCES

Cooper, W. E. (1982). Time management techniques for clinicians. In P. A. Keller & L. G. Ritt (Eds.), *Innovations in clinical practice: A source book* (pp. 177–183). Sarasota, FL: Professional Resource Exchange.

Dhooper, S. S., Huff, M. B., & Schultz, C. M. (1989). Social work and sexual harassment. *Journal of Sociology and Social Welfare, 16*(3), 125–138.

Fortune, A. E., Feathers, C. E., Rook, S. R., Scrimenti, R., Smollen, O., Stemerman, B., & Tucker, E. (1985). Student satisfaction with field placement. *Journal of Social Work Education, 21*(3), 92–104.

Gabel, S., Oster, G., & Pfeffer, C. R. (1988). *Difficult moments in child psychiatry.* New York: Plenum Medical.

James, J. (1981). Sexual harassment. *Public Personnel Management Journal, 10*(4), 402–407.

Johnston, N., Rooney, R., & Reitmeir, M. A. (1991). Sharing power: Student feedback to field supervisors. In D. Schneck, B. Grossman, & U. Glasman (Eds.), *Field education in social work: Contemporary issues and trends.* Dubuque, IA: Kendall/Hunt.

Pope, K. S. (1986). Research and laws regarding therapist–patient sexual involvement: Implications for therapists. *American Journal of Psychotherapy, 40*(4), 564–571.

Pope, K. S., Simpson, N. H. & Weiner, M. F. (1978). Malpractice in outpatient psychotherapy. *American Journal of Psychotherapy, 32*(4), 593–602.

Schubert, M. (1982). *Interviewing in social work practice: An introduction.* New York: Council on Social Work Education.

ADDITIONAL READINGS

Corey, G., Corey, M., & Callanan, P. (1988). *Issues and ethics in the helping professions.* Pacific Grove, CA: Brooks/Cole.

Gelman, S. R., & Wardell, P. J. (1988). Who's responsible? The field liability dilemma. *Journal of Social Work Education, 24*(1), 70–78.

Lakein, A. (1974). *How to get control of your time and your life.* New York: New American Library.

Loewenberg, F., & Dolgoff, R. (1988). *Ethical decisions for social work practice.* Itasca, IL: F. E. Peacock.

Reamer, F. G. (1983). Ethical dilemmas in social work practice. *Social Work, 28*(1), 31–35.

Rhodes, M. L. (1986). *Ethical dilemmas in social work practice.* London: Routledge & Kegan Paul.

Rogers, C. (1957). The necessary and sufficient conditions of therapeutic personality change. *Journal of Consulting Psychology, 21*(2), 95–103.

Sanford, W. (1981). *Fighting sexual harassment: An advocacy handbook.* Boston: Alyson Publications & Alliance Against Sexual Coercion.

Wells, C. C., & Masch, M. K. (1986). *Social work ethics day to day: Guidelines for professional practice.* White Plains, NY: Longman.

APPENDIX **A**

Problem-Oriented Recording

Record-keeping today involves a complex series of decisions in which social work agencies have to balance the costs of detailed reporting systems against their benefits. How much information and what information should become part of the official record? What information is pertinent and what is immaterial? More comprehensive records generally allow greater accountability but are costlier to maintain and may provide less protection of the client's confidentiality.

Information in ongoing records must be organized in some logical, coherent manner, and social service agencies have tackled this problem in a number of ways. One approach, the problem-oriented record (also known as the problem-oriented medical record, the problem-goal-oriented record, the problem-oriented system, or the Weed system), has been widely adopted by agencies in health and human service settings. This approach has been described as having a "remarkable concurrence with and support of social work principles and functions" (Biagi, 1977 p. 212).

The problem-oriented record has four components: (1) a data base that contains relevant information about the client; (2) a problem list that includes a statement of initial complaints; (3) an assessment and plan related to each identified problem; and (4) progress notes about what was done and the outcome of each activity.

There are several variations of the problem-oriented record. Perhaps the most often used form is SOAP. For each identified problem, the social worker records *subjective* information (the client's perception of the problem), *objective* information (the facts of the case; information that can be verified), the *assessment* (the professional's conclusions about the nature of the problem), and the *plan* for intervention. Another variation is PAP (*problem, assessment, plan*), in which the client's subjective complaint and the objective information pertaining to the problem are brought together. The assessment and plan portions of PAP remain the same as in SOAP.

Tremendous diversity exists in social service agencies, particularly in the ways that they are organized and run. In fact, the way in which your practicum agency wants you to record client data in its files may not look at all like the SOAP or PAP systems. Sometimes other organizational schemes form the basis for documenting pertinent client information in the agency's records. For instance, some of the data may be organized using Perlman's (1957) *4-Ps (person, problem, place,* and *process)* or Doremus' (1976) *4-Rs (roles, reactions, relationships,* and *resources).* You may discover many variations of these schemes as you are placed in different social service agencies.

REFERENCES

Biagi, E. (1977). The social work stake in problem-oriented recording. *Social Work in Health Care, 3*(2), 211–221.

Doremus, B. (1976, July). The four R's: Social diagnosis in health care. *Health and Social Work, 23,* 296–299.

Perlman, H. (1957). *Social casework: A problem-solving process.* Chicago: University of Chicago Press.

ADDITIONAL READINGS

Burke, P. C. (1988). Consultation and the use of policy guidelines in case recording. *Social Work Education, 7*(3), 7–11.

Hartman, B. L., & Wickey, J. M. (1978, July). The person-oriented record in treatment. *Social Work, 23,* 296–299.

Johnson, H. C. (1978). Integrating the problem-oriented record with a systems approach to case assessment. *Journal of Education for Social Work, 14*(3), 71–77.

Kane, R. A. (1974). Look to the record. *Social Work, 19*(4), 412–419.

Vickar, G. M., & Herjanic, M. (1976). The use of problem-oriented medical records in community mental health centers. *American Journal of Psychiatry, 133*(3), 340–341.

Weed, L. L. (1969). *Medical records, medical education and patient care.* Cleveland, OH: Case Western Reserve University.

National Association of Social Workers Code of Ethics

I. *The Social Worker's Conduct and Comportment as a Social Worker*

A. *Propriety*—The social worker should maintain high standards of personal conduct in the capacity or identity as social worker.

   1. The private conduct of the social worker is a personal matter to the same degree as is any other person's, except when such conduct compromises the fulfillment of professional responsibilities.
   2. The social worker should not participate in, condone, or be associated with dishonesty, fraud, deceit, or misrepresentation.
   3. The social worker should distinguish clearly between statements and actions made as a private individual and as a representative of the social work profession or an organization or group.

B. *Competence and Professional Development*—The social worker should strive to become and remain proficient in professional practice and the performance of professional functions.

   1. The social worker should accept responsibility or employment only on the basis of existing competence or the intention to acquire the necessary competence.
   2. The social worker should not misrepresent professional qualifications, education, experience, or affiliations.

C. *Service*—The social worker should regard as primary the service obligation of the social work profession.

   1. The social worker should retain ultimate responsibility for the quality and extent of the service that individual assumes, assigns, or performs.
   2. The social worker should act to prevent practices that are inhumane or discriminatory against any person or group of persons.

D. *Integrity*—The social worker should act in accordance with the highest standards of professional integrity and impartiality.

1. The social worker should be alert to and resist the influences and pressures that interfere with the exercise of professional discretion and impartial judgment required for the performance of professional functions.

2. The social worker should not exploit professional relationships for personal gain.

E. *Scholarship and Research*—The social worker engaged in study and research should be guided by the conventions of scholarly inquiry.

1. The social worker engaged in research should consider carefully its possible consequences for human beings.

2. The social worker engaged in research should ascertain that the consent of participants in the research is voluntary and informed without any implied deprivation or penalty for refusal to participate, and with due regard for participants' privacy and dignity.

3. The social worker engaged in research should protect participants from unwarranted physical or mental discomfort, distress, harm, danger, or deprivation.

4. The social worker who engages in the evaluation of services or cases should discuss them only for professional purposes and only with persons directly and professionally concerned with them.

5. Information obtained about participants in research should be treated as confidential.

6. The social worker should take credit only for work actually done in connection with scholarly and research endeavors and credit contributions made by others.

II. *The Social Worker's Ethical Responsibility to Clients*

F. *Primacy of Clients' Interests*—The social worker's primary responsibility is to clients.

1. The social worker should serve clients with devotion, loyalty, determination, and the maximum application of professional skill and competence.

2. The social worker should not exploit relationships with clients for personal advantage, or solicit the clients of one's agency for private practice.

3. The social worker should not practice, condone, facilitate, or collaborate with any form of discrimination on the basis of race, color, sex, sexual orientation, age, religion, national origin, marital status, political belief, mental or physical handicap, or any other preference or personal characteristic, condition, or status.

4. The social worker should avoid relationships or commitments that conflict with the interests of clients.

5. The social worker should under no circumstances engage in sexual activities with clients.

6. The social worker should provide clients with accurate and complete information regarding the extent and nature of the services available to them.
7. The social worker should apprise clients of their risks, rights, opportunities, and obligations associated with social service to them.
8. The social worker should seek advice and counsel of colleagues and supervisors whenever such consultation is in the best interest of clients.
9. The social worker should terminate service to clients, and professional relationships with them, when such service and relationships are no longer required or no longer serve the clients' needs or interests.
10. The social worker should withdraw services precipitously only under unusual circumstances, giving careful consideration to all factors in the situation and taking care to minimize possible adverse effects.
11. The social worker who anticipates the termination or interruption of service to clients should notify clients promptly and seek the transfer, referral, or continuation of services in relation to the clients' needs and preferences.

G. *Rights and Prerogatives of Clients*—The social worker should make every effort to foster maximum self-determination on the part of clients.
1. When the social worker must act on behalf of a client who has been adjudged legally incompetent, the social worker should safeguard the interests and rights of the client.
2. When another individual has been legally authorized to act on behalf of a client, the social worker should deal with that person always with the client's best interest in mind.
3. The social worker should not engage in any action that violates or diminishes the civil or legal rights of clients.

H. *Confidentiality and Privacy*—The social worker should respect the privacy of clients and hold in confidence all information obtained in the course of professional service.
1. The social worker should share with others confidences revealed by clients without their consent, only for compelling professional reasons.
2. The social worker should inform clients fully about the limits of confidentiality in a given situation, the purposes for which information is obtained, and how it may be used.
3. The social worker should afford clients reasonable access to any official social work records concerning them.
4. When providing clients with access to records, the social worker should take due care to protect the confidences of others contained in those records.
5. The social worker should obtain informed consent of clients before taping, recording, or permitting third party observation of their activities.

I. Fees—When setting fees, the social worker should ensure that they are fair, reasonable, considerate, and commensurate with the service performed and with due regard for the client's ability to pay.

   1. The social worker should not divide a fee or accept or give anything of value for receiving or making a referral.

III. The Social Worker's Ethical Responsibility to Colleagues

J. Respect, Fairness, and Courtesy—The social worker should treat colleagues with respect, courtesy, fairness, and good faith.

   1. The social worker should cooperate with colleagues to promote professional interests and concerns.
   2. The social worker should respect confidences shared by colleagues in the course of their professional relationships and transactions.
   3. The social worker should create and maintain conditions of practice that facilitate ethical and competent professional performance by colleagues.
   4. The social worker should treat with respect, and represent accurately and fairly, the qualifications, views, and findings of colleagues and use appropriate channels to express judgements on these matters.
   5. The social worker who replaces or is replaced by a colleague in professional practice should act with consideration for the interest, character, and reputation of that colleague.
   6. The social worker should not exploit a dispute between a colleague and employers to obtain a position or otherwise advance the social worker's interest.
   7. The social worker should seek arbitration or mediation when conflicts with colleagues require resolution for compelling professional reasons.
   8. The social worker should extend to colleagues of other professions the same respect and cooperation that is extended to social work colleagues.
   9. The social worker who serves as an employer, supervisor, or mentor to colleagues should make orderly and explicit arrangements regarding the conditions of their professional relationship.
   10. The social worker who has the responsibility for employing and evaluating the performance of other staff memebers should fulfill such responsibility in a fair, considerate, and equitable manner, on the basis of clearly enunciated criteria.
   11. The social worker who has the responsibility for evaluating the performance of employees, supervisees, or students should share evaluations with them.

K. Dealing with Colleagues' Clients—The social worker has the responsibility to relate to the clients of colleagues with full professional consideration.

   1. The social worker should not solicit the clients of colleagues.
   2. The social worker should not assume professional responsibility for the clients of another agency or a colleague without appropriate communication with that agency or colleague.

3. The social worker who serves the clients of colleagues, during a temporary absence or emergency, should serve those clients with the same consideration as that afforded any client.

IV. *The Social Worker's Ethical Responsibility to Employers and Employing Organizations*

L. *Commitments to Employing Organization*—The social worker should adhere to commitments made to the employing organization.

1. The social worker should work to improve the employing agency's policies and procedures, and the efficiency and effectiveness of its services.
2. The social worker should not accept employment or arrange student field placements in an organization which is currently under public sanction by NASW for violating personnel standards, or imposing limitations on or penalties for professional actions on behalf of clients.
3. The social worker should act to prevent and eliminate discrimination in the employing organization's work assignments and in its employment policies and practices.
4. The social worker should use with scrupulous regard, and only for the purpose for which they are intended, the resources of the employing organization.

V. *The Social Worker's Ethical Responsibility to the Social Work Profession*

M. *Maintaining the Integrity of the Profession*—The social worker should uphold and advance the values, ethics, knowledge, and mission of the profession.

1. The social worker should protect and enhance the dignity and integrity of the profession and should be responsible and vigorous in discussion and criticism of the profession.
2. The social worker should take action through appropriate channels against unethical conduct by any other member of the profession.
3. The social worker should act to prevent the unauthorized and unqualified practice of social work.
4. The social worker should make no misrepresentation in advertising as to qualifications, competence, service, or results to be achieved.

N. *Community Service*—The social worker should assist the profession in making social services available to the general public.

1. The social worker should contribute time and professional expertise to activities that promote respect for the utility, the integrity, and the competence of the social work profession.
2. The social worker should support the formulation, development, enactment, and implementation of social policies of concern to the profession.

O. *Development of Knowledge*—The social worker should take responsibility for identifying, developing, and fully utilizing knowledge for professional practice.

1. The social worker should base practice upon recognized knowledge relevant to social work.
2. The social worker should critically examine, and keep current with, emerging knowledge relevant to social work.
3. The social worker should contribute to the knowledge base of social work and share research knowledge and practice wisdom with colleagues.

VI. *The Social Worker's Ethical Responsibility to Society*

P. *Promoting the General Welfare*—The social worker should promote the general welfare of society.

1. The social worker should act to prevent and eliminate discrimination against any person or group on the basis of race, color, sex, sexual orientation, age, religion, national origin, marital status, political belief, mental or physical handicap, or any other preference or personal characteristic, condition, or status.
2. The social worker should act to ensure that all persons have access to the resources, services, and opportunities which they require.
3. The social worker should act to expand choice and opportunity for all persons, with special regard for disadvantaged or oppressed groups and persons.
4. The social worker should promote conditions that encourage respect for the diversity of cultures which constitute American society.
5. The social worker should provide appropriate professional services in public emergencies.
6. The social worker should advocate changes in policy and legislation to improve social conditions and to promote social justice.
7. The social worker should encourage informed participation by the public in shaping social policies and institutions.

Index